GERMAN IMPERIALISM, 1914–1918:
The Development of a Historical Debate

MAJOR ISSUES IN HISTORY

Editor

C. WARREN HOLLISTER

University of California, Santa Barbara

GERMAN IMPERIALISM, 1914–1918:

The Development of a Historical Debate

EDITED BY

Gerald D. Feldman

University of California at Berkeley

John Wiley & Sons, Inc.,

New York • London • Sydney • Toronto

Library of Congress Catalogue Card Number: 73-38964

Printed in the United States of America.

10 9 8 7 6 5 4 3 2 1

Library of Congress Cataloging in Publication Data

Feldman, Gerald D., comp.
    German imperialism, 1914–1918.

    (Major issues in history)
    Bibliography: p.
    1. European War, 1914–1918—Germany. 2. European War, 1914–1918—Sources. 3. European War, 1914–1918—Peace. I. Title.
D515.F24   943.08'4   73-38964
ISBN 0-471-25702-8
ISBN 0-471-25703-6 (pbk.)

SERIES PREFACE

The reading program in a history survey course traditionally has consisted of a large two-volume textbook and, perhaps, a book of readings. This simple reading program requires few decisions and little imagination on the instructor's part, and tends to encourage in the student the virtue of careful memorization. Such programs are by no means things of the past, but they certainly do not represent the wave of the future.

The reading program in survey courses at many colleges and universities today is far more complex. At the risk of oversimplification, and allowing for many exceptions and overlaps, it can be divided into four categories: (1) textbook, (2) original source readings, (3) specialized historical essays and interpretive studies, and (4) historical problems.

After obtaining an overview of the course subject matter (textbook), sampling the original sources, and being exposed to selective examples of excellent modern historical writing (historical essays), the student can turn to the crucial task of weighing various possible interpretations of major historical issues. It is at this point that memory gives way to creative critical thought. The "problems approach," in other words, is the intellectual climax of a thoughtfully conceived reading program and is, indeed, the most characteristic of all approaches to historical pedagogy among the newer generation of college and university teachers.

The historical problems books currently available are many and varied. Why add to this information explosion? Because the Wiley Major Issues Series constitutes an endeavor to produce something new that will respond to pedagogical needs thus far unmet. First, it is a series of individual volumes—one per problem. Many good teachers would much prefer to select their own historical issues rather than be tied to an inflexible sequence of issues imposed by a publisher and bound together between two covers. Second, the Wiley Major Issues Series is based on the idea of approaching the significant problems of history through a deft interweaving of primary sources and secondary analysis, fused together by the skill of a scholar-editor. It is felt that the essence of a historical issue cannot be satisfactorily probed either

by placing a body of undigested source materials into the hands
of inexperienced students or by limiting these students to the
controversial literature of modern scholars who debate the meaning of sources the student never sees. This series approaches
historical problems by exposing students to both the finest historical thinking on the issue and some of the evidence on which
this thinking is based. This synthetic approach should prove far
more fruitful than either the raw-source approach or the exclusively second-hand approach, for it combines the advantages—
and avoids the serious disadvantage—of both.

Finally, the editors of the individual volumes in the Major
Issues Series have been chosen from among the ablest scholars in
their fields. Rather than faceless referees, they are historians who
know their issues from the inside and, in most instances, have
themselves contributed significantly to the relevant scholarly
literature. It has been the editorial policy of this series to permit
the editor-scholars of the individual volumes the widest possible
latitude both in formulating their topics and in organizing their
materials. Their scholarly competence has been unquestioningly
respected; they have been encouraged to approach the problems
as they see fit. The titles and themes of the series volumes have
been suggested in nearly every case by the scholar-editors themselves. The criteria have been (1) that the issue be of relevance
to undergraduate lecture courses in history, and (2) that it be an
issue which the scholar-editor knows thoroughly and in which
he has done creative work. And, in general, the second criterion
has been given precedence over the first. In short, the question
"What are the significant historical issues today?" has been
answered not by general editors or sales departments but by the
scholar-teachers who are responsible for these volumes.

University of California,   *C. Warren Hollister*
Santa Barbara

CONTENTS

INTRODUCTION

PART ONE

Pre-1945 Documents and Interpretations:

A. The Sources

PART TWO

Post-1945 Documents and Interpretations:

B.   The Interpretations

INTRODUCTION

European diplomatic history between 1890 and 1945 is dominated largely by the problem of German imperialism. It is well to remember, however, how relatively sudden and swift was Germany's rise and fall as a power capable of large-scale aggression. Until her unification under Prussian leadership in 1871, there was not even a state, let alone a great power, called Germany. Furthermore, few historians would contest that the German Empire under Bismarck's chancellorship (1871–1890) pursued a foreign policy aimed at stabilizing international relations on the European continent and achieving relatively limited gains in the European scramble for colonies abroad. Although there were political and social groups within Germany seeking to burst the bonds of Bismarck's restraining foreign policy, their tangible successes during his regime were limited to a brief spurt of colonial expansion in 1884–1885. It was not until the fall of Bismarck in 1890 and the gradual redirection of German foreign policy under the aegis of Kaiser William II (1888–1918) that Germany embarked on that program of "world policy" (*Weltpolitik*), fleet building, and belligerence that played such a major role in bringing about the First World War. Germany's defeat and the humiliating Treaty of Versailles, which her enemies imposed on her in 1919, necessarily constituted an external brake on German imperialism, although the proponents of a greater Germany did not cease to promote their ideas during the ill-fated Weimar Republic (1918–1933). The seizure of power by Adolph Hitler in 1933 opened the way to the final German imperialist effort which culminated in the Nazi barbarities of the Second World War (1939–1945) and which led to the total defeat and present-day division of Germany.

The rubble left by the catastrophe of 1945 is almost entirely cleared away, but the historical problems raised by Germany's imperialist ventures remain vexing and are difficult to bring into satisfactory focus. Few historical issues have attracted more attention, debate, and even acrimony in recent years, for example, than the subject of this book, German war aims in the First World War. On the surface, this would seem surprising, since there has never been much mystery about the content of German ambitions between 1914 and 1918. If Germany had won a total victory, there can be no question about the fact that she would have expanded her boundaries, power, and influence in Europe and the world. In the west, Germany would have controlled Belgium, whose neutrality she violated in August 1914, by a combination of direct annexations of strategically important regions and control over the economic and political life of a rump Belgian state. France would have lost the rich iron ore region of Briey-Longwy, and the Franco-German border would have been "rectified" for strategic reasons. An indemnity would have been imposed on France and England, and both powers would have been compelled to surrender substantial colonial areas to Germany. These ambitions went unrealized but, if proof be needed of Germany's will to realize her goals, it can be found in the Treaty of Brest-Litovsk imposed on Russia in March 1918. Under the guise of "self-determination," this treaty deprived Russia of the Ukraine, the Baltic states, and the Russian portion of Poland. It gave Germany *de facto* political and economic hegemony to supplement the hegemony that she had already established in Central Europe (*Mitteleuropa*) through the control she exerted over her weak allies, Austria-Hungary and Bulgaria, and over her defeated enemy, Rumania. Given the evidence and the record, why should Germany's aims in the First World War provoke so much controversy among historians?

As this anthology attempts to show, Germany's war aims have raised a host of problems whose terms have been defined by changing perspectives and new evidence. From the very outset, two aspects of the war aims problem have been sources of contention. First, it has been argued that Germany's war aims cannot be considered in isolation. Her enemies also had imperialist goals. France desired to recover Alsace-Lorraine and separate the Rhineland from Germany. Russia sought control of the Straits of Constantinople, domination of the Balkans and a revision of her western borders at the expense of Germany. England wished to destroy Germany's naval power and take Germany's colonies. Italy, like her allies, wished to participate in the carving up of the Ottoman Empire and had territorial ambitions in the Tyrol and portions of the Austro-Hungarian Empire which are now parts of Yugoslavia. These Allied war aims were set down in secret treaties published by the Bolsheviks after they took power in 1917, and the publication did a splendid job of proving the Bolshevik contention that the First World War was an imperialist war on all sides. Furthermore, the Treaty of Versailles, even if it did not realize all the ambitions of the Allies, was sufficiently harsh to demonstrate that Germany was not the only power capable of imposing a Carthaginian peace. In short, from the perspective of Allied war aims, German aims could be found less astonishing, and an argument could even be made that they were a reaction to the "encirclement" of Germany by her rapacious enemies. The existence of extensive Allied war aims does not disprove the existence or diminish the significance of Germany's goals, but they do raise the problem of the perspective from which they are to be viewed.

The second issue that has arisen continuously in the war aims discussion has been that of who the annexationists really were. It must be remembered that Germany did not win the total victory expected at the beginning of the war and that some German leaders recognized the need to modify their country's war aims. To what extent was the German government willing to sacrifice German ambitions to achieve peace, and to what extent did German inability or unwillingness to sacrifice her war aims prolong the war? There has been general agreement that the military authorities, especially the Supreme Commanders, Field Marshal Paul von Hindenburg and First Quartermaster General Erich Ludendorff, who took office in August 1916, supported extreme war aims and exerted incredible pressure on the government to continue the war until these aims were achieved. In this demand they were allied with the war aims movement directed by extremist organizations like the Pan-German League and influential business and agrarian groups. Opposition to the extremists came from moderate and left wing groups and political parties, above all the Majority Socialists, who supported the war effort but opposed annexationism, and the Independent Socialists, who refused to vote for war credits and insisted on a peace without annexations and indemnities. The responsible civilian leadership of the empire, above all Germany's major wartime Chancellor, Theobold von Bethmann Hollweg (1909–1917), had the difficult task of directing German foreign policy in the midst of this fierce domestic conflict over war aims. As is well recognized, there were serious disputes between Bethmann and the Supreme Command. The latter found Bethmann's commitment to an annexationist peace to be weak and had to force the Chancellor to introduce unrestricted submarine warfare in January 1917. Bethmann's justified fear that the U-boats would bring America into the war was brushed aside by the Supreme Command, as was Bethmann's apparent concern over the outcome of the war. In July 1917, the Supreme Command succeeded in having Bethmann dismissed, and this was followed by a "Ludendorff dictatorship" in matters of foreign policy. Nevertheless, civilian-military conflicts over the means, and perhaps some of the ends, of German policy continued. The civilian leaders seemed more moderate than the military, but how "moderate" was their moderation? Where did the civilian leaders, especially Bethmann Hollweg, really stand? Finally, what was the relationship between domestic and foreign affairs; that is, to what extent did the political lineup on sociopolitical issues like reform of the plutocratic Prussian suffrage system and the introduction of ministerial responsibility to parliament, parallel and influence the lineup on the war aims question? As shall be seen, opponents of political reform tended to support annexationist war aims just as proponents of a peace of understanding tended to want reform at home. The question of who the annexationists really were leads directly to the problem of the relationship between Germany's domestic structure and her foreign policy.

The above discussed aspects of the war aims problem, which were recognized by historians from the very outset of the debate, do not end the complexities of this issue. History is a living subject, and historical questions take on new meaning and significance as a result of new historical developments. The Second World War forced historians to take another look at its predecessor. Hitler's barbaric pursuit of "Living Space" (*Lebensraum*) in the east placed the earlier controversies about Germany's aims in the First World War in a new light and made them more compelling. Was Hitler's quest for *Lebensraum* in eastern Europe and the hegemony he established for Germany in central and western Europe in any sense a continuation of fundamental tendencies in German imperialism that were already evident in the First World War and, perhaps, even before 1914? Was there a direct line between William II and Hitler? It now seemed possible to investigate such questions very thoroughly because when Germany lost the Second World War she also lost control of the enormous documentary files of the Imperial German Foreign Office as well as other government agencies. Unhappily, it was soon discovered that vast quantities of new evidence and information can make the task of interpretation harder rather than easier.

This is particularly true when the historical problem is emotionally charged. Wartime propagandists and anti-German writers have often insisted that German history is all of a piece, while apologists for Germany usually argue that Hitler's imperialism was unique and that Nazism itself was an accident or deviation from the normal course of German history. Conservative German historians have been prepared to accept a relationship between Pan-Germanism, Ludendorff, and Hitler, but they have argued that the true representative of the Second Empire was Ludendorff's victim, Bethmann Hollweg. This happy solution to a very distressing dilemma was seriously challenged in 1961 when the Hamburg historian, Professor Fritz Fischer, published his *Griff nach der Weltmacht* (translated as *Germany's Aims in the First World War*). Basing his massive study on years of archival research, Fischer concluded that there was little distinction between the war aims of a Bethmann Hollweg and a Ludendorff. The major differences, such as they were, were above all differences of nuance, of means rather than ends. Most important, Fischer sought to establish the continuity of German aims from prewar to wartime imperialism and dared to suggest that the continuity did not end there.

Fischer's conclusions were greeted with mutterings of "treason" and sharp criticism from important segments of the German historical guild. His most famous opponent, the eminent Professor Gerhard Ritter, did not limit himself to factual refutations of Fischer and called Fischer's book an example of the "self-deprecation of the German historical consciousness." Irrelevant charges like these demonstrated how relevant the issues raised by Fischer were. During the past few years, however, some of the smoke has cleared and the discussion has been freed of a good deal of the emotion that obscured rather than illuminated the issues. Criticism of Fischer continues, but there is a measure of consensus among historians that annexationism was more widely

spread and more continuously supported than had previously
been supposed and that the traditional view of Bethmann Hollweg needs some revision. Similarly, although historians remain
unclear about the precise connection between German imperialism in 1911, 1914, and 1939, there is an increasing willingness to
recognize the validity of the problem when stated this way. In
short, Fischer, like any good historian, has solved some problems but has opened up a great many more.

The organization of this book is designed to illustrate the
history of the German war aims problem both in terms of the
discovery of evidence and in terms of the actual discussion of this
evidence by historians. Part One is devoted to the pre-1945
period; Part Two deals with materials and historical writings
that have appeared since 1945. The fact that Part One contains
a larger number of selections than Part Two is misleading, since
it must be borne in mind that the amount of documentary material made available since 1945 literally exceeds what was previously at the historian's disposal by hundreds of thousands of
pages. A better perspective on the state and character of the evidence may be attained if one is aware that most of the material
available before 1945 came from published sources: newspaper
reports, pamphlets, and the Reichstag debates. The only archival
documents made available were those provided by official government agencies, usually for propagandistic reasons, and the documents used by the historians who served as experts for the official
Reichstag Investigation Committee investigating the origins of
the collapse of 1918. These constituted a pitifully small segment
of what was lying in the archives, as the opening of the archives
after 1945 clearly demonstrated. Thus, although very few of the
documents presented in Part One are taken from archival sources,
all those presented in Part Two are archival documents. The latter have been chosen to illustrate the types of new evidence available rather to reveal their enormous bulk. An additional objective
of this book is to give the reader a sense of the substantial historical literature that has emerged from the research into this material and of the degree to which new historical evidence can both
assist and hinder the historian in his search for the answer to basic
problems of historical interpretation.

PART ONE

Pre-1945 Documents and Interpretations
A. The Sources

1   *William II's Speech from the*
Throne, August 4, 1914

If the Kaiser's speech to the assembled representatives of the
people is a piece of war propaganda, it nevertheless is a signifi-
cant one. His presentation of the origins of the war, particularly
his emphasis on Russia's responsibility, was given almost univer-
sal credibility in Germany. It was exceptionally important in
rallying the Social Democrats to the war effort since they loathed
autocratic Russia but were by no means enthusiastic about fight-
ing France and England. Russia's alleged war guilt combined
with the assurances that Germany was not fighting for conquests
served to rally the workers to the war effort and establish the so-
called "Truce of the Fortress" (Burgfrieden) which was meant
to suspend political conflict for the duration of the war.

"Honored gentlemen, at a time of such importance I have assembled the elected representatives of the German people about
me. For nearly half a century we have been allowed to follow the
ways of peace. The attempts to attribute to Germany warlike intentions and to hedge in her position in the world have often

SOURCE (1). Reprinted from *Fall of the German Empire,* 1914–1918, Volume
I, pp. 8–9, edited by Ralph Haswell Lutz, with the permission of the publishers, Stanford University Press. Copyright 1932 by the Board of Trustees
of the Leland Stanford Junior University.

sorely tried the patience of my people. Undeterred, my Government has pursued the development of our moral, spiritual, and economic strength as its highest aim, with all frankness, even under provocative circumstances. The world has been witness that during the last years, under all pressure and confusion, we have stood in the first rank in saving the nations of Europe from a war between the great powers.

"The most serious dangers to which the events in the Balkans had given rise seemed to have been overcome—then suddenly an abyss was opened through the murder of my friend the Archduke Franz Ferdinand. My lofty ally, the Emperor and King Franz Josef, was forced to take up arms to defend the security of his empire against dangerous machinations from a neighboring state. The Russian Empire stepped in to hinder the allied monarchy from following out her just interests. Not only does our duty as ally call us to the side of Austria-Hungary, but it is our great task to protect our own position and the old community of culture between the two Empires against the attack of hostile forces.

"With a heavy heart I have had to mobilize the army against a neighbor with whom it had fought side by side on many a battlefield. With unfeigned sorrow I saw broken a friendship which had been faithfully preserved by Germany. The Imperial Russian Government, yielding to the pressure of an insatiable nationalism, has taken sides with a state which through its sanctioning of criminal attacks has brought the evils of this war. That France, too, should have taken sides with our enemy could not surprise us; too often have attempts to come to a more friendly relationship with the French Republic failed because of her old hopes and old resentments.

"Honored gentlemen, what human insight and power could do to equip a people for these uttermost decisions has been done with your patriotic assistance. The hostility which has been making itself felt in the East and in the West for a long time past has now broken out in bright flame. The present situation is the result of an ill will which has been active for many years against the power and the prosperity of the German Empire.

"No lust of conquest drives us on; we are inspired by the unalterable will to protect the place in which God has set us for ourselves and all coming generations. From the documents which have been submitted to you, you will see how my Government, and especially my Chancellor, have endeavored even to the last moment to stave off the inevitable. In a defensive war that has been forced upon us, with a clear conscience and a clean hand we take up the sword.

"I issue my call to the peoples and stocks of the German Empire that with their united strength they may stand like brothers with our allies in order to defend what we have created through the works of peace. Following the example of our fathers, staunch and true, earnest and knightly, humble before God, but with the joy of battle in the face of the enemy, we trust in the Almighty to strengthen our defense and guide us to good issue.

"Honored gentlemen, the German people gathered about their princes and leaders are today looking to you. Come to your decisions quickly and unanimously. Such is my most earnest wish."

His Majesty added to that:

"You have read, gentlemen, what I have said to my people from the balcony of the castle. Here I repeat: I know no more parties, I only know Germans. [*Loud cheers.*] As proof that you are strongly resolved to hold with me, through thick and thin, through want until death, without difference of race and difference of religion, I challenge the leaders of the parties to step forward and to pledge me their word."

The leaders of the parties did so under loud and protracted applause. Thereupon the Chancellor stepped forward and declared the Reichstag opened.

After renewed cheers, uttered by the Bavarian Minister von Lerchenfeld-Köfering and in which he was joined by the others, the assembly sang with enthusiasm "Heil Dir im Siegerkranz," to which the Kaiser listened standing. Amidst continued cheers His Majesty left the hall with a "Thank you" to all sides, and shaking hands with many members as he left.

2 FROM   *Bethmann Hollweg's Speech to
the Reichstag, August 4, 1914*

*One of the least happy consequences of the German military
authorities' independence of civilian and parliamentary control
was the political ineptness and inflexibility of the General Staff's
planning for the war. In 1914 Germany had only one plan in the
event of war, the Schlieffen Plan, which was based on the assumption that Germany could not afford to fight a long war and that
her best chances lay in a speedy defeat of France followed by a
concentration on Russia. Rapid victory over France required the
circumvention of the French fortresses, and this could only be
achieved by the invasion of neutral Belgium. As it turned out,
the Schlieffen Plan failed, and the Germans were stopped on the
Marne in September 1914. The invasion of Belgium, however,
enabled the British government to gain mass support for its decision to fight Germany. Bethmann's remarks concerning Belgium are particularly interesting in the light of the subsequent
development of German plans for the future of Belgium.*

. . . Gentlemen, we are now in a state of necessity (*Notwehr*)
[*lively approval*], and necessity (*Not*) knows no law. [*Stormy applause.*] Our troops have occupied Luxemburg [*applause*] and
perhaps have already entered Belgian territory. [*Renewed applause.*]

Gentlemen, that is a breach of international law. [*"Hear! hear!"
—Right.*] It is true that the French Government declared at Brussels that France would respect Belgian neutrality as long as her
adversary respected it. We knew, however, that France stood ready
for an invasion. [*"Hear! hear!"—Right.*] France could wait; we
could not. A French attack on our flank on the lower Rhine

SOURCE (2). Reprinted from *Fall of the German Empire, 1914–1918,* Volume
I. pp. 12–13, edited by Ralph Haswell Lutz, with the permission of the publishers, Stanford University Press. Copyright 1932 by the Board of Trustees
of the Leland Stanford Junior University.

might have been disastrous. [*Lively approval.*] Thus we were forced to ignore the rightful protests of the Governments of Luxemburg and Belgium. [*"Quite right!"*] The wrong—I speak openly—the wrong we thereby commit we will try to make good as soon as our military aims have been attained. [*Applause.*]

He who is menaced as we are and is fighting for his highest possession can only consider how he is to hack his way through (*durchhauen*). [*Enthusiastic applause in entire House.*] . . .

3 FROM *Memorandum of the Secretaries of the Interior and the Foreign Office on the Belgian Question, December 31, 1914*

Despite Bethmann's admission of the wrong done to Belgium and his promise to restore and compensate that country, German ambitions in Belgium found early and very concrete expression at the highest levels of the government. The fulfillment of the program outlined in this memorandum is made contingent upon a "decisive German victory." Nevertheless, even the most pro-German historians have been critical of Germany's unwillingness to make a clear public statement of her intentions toward Belgium, a statement repudiating the kind of intentions presented in this memorandum. The document was taken from the archives by Erich Otto Volkmann and was published as an appendix to his report for the Reichstag Investigating Committee.

SOURCE (3). Translated by the editor from *Die Ursachen des Deutschen Zusammenbruches im Jahre 1918. Das Werk des Untersuchungsausschusses der Verfassunggebenden Deutschen Reichstages 1918–1928* (hereafter cited as *Ursachen*), Berlin, Deutsche Verlagsgesellschaft fur Politik und Geschichte m.b. H., 1929, Vol. 12, Part I, pp. 193–199.

Berlin, December 31, 1914

TOP SECRET

. . . If it should transpire that the present war ends with a decisive victory for German arms, then we should consider the possibility of resurrecting Belgium as a tributary state in such a way that it would be placed at the military as well as economic disposal of the Reich but would in form remain as free as possible and not burden us with the political executive.

I. The Military Security of Belgium

Belgium must be made so secure for us that in a future war it would not be in the position of serving the enemy as a base for his operations.

1. Such security presupposes that the fortresses, the coasts, and the means of transportation actually are controlled by Germany. . . .
2. The military security of Belgium, however, is only further possible if Belgium is not permitted to have its own army under its own military sovereignty. . . .
3. The right of military occupation in Belgium necessarily brings with it a number of other restrictions on Belgian sovereignty.

> (a) It will not do to have the German occupation troops subjected to Belgian justice, for it will take on a strongly chauvinistic character after the war because of the embitterment of the population against the Germans. . . . Consequently, the German occupation must be placed under the authority of its own judiciary. . . .
>
> (b) A secure military control of Belgium is out of the question so long as the Belgian Government can conduct its own foreign policy. For by means of uncontrolled intercourse with powers hostile to us, the Belgian Government will be in a position to conspire persistently against us and cut across our foreign policy, and also to reach an understanding with our enemy such as to threaten our military security

by means of a popular uprising in an emergency.

(aa) Accordingly, Belgium must give over its right of international representation to the Government of the Reich.

(bb) It should not be allowed to have ambassadors to foreign powers. . . .

(cc) Even the right to its own consular representation cannot be accorded Belgium because it is to be expected that the Belgian government, desirous of liberation from German influence, will use the consular officials as diplomatic representatives. Insofar, therefore, as an independent Belgian commercial flag continues to be flown, it would be protected by our consular representatives.

(c) An independent colonial policy will be impossible for Belgium under these conditions. The protection of the Congo State, internally and externally, must also be turned over to the Reich.

(d) In the domestic administration of Belgium the Reich is to be reserved a right of veto over all laws and administrative measures which threaten to harm our military interests. Particularly the regulation of the relationship between the police and military administrations will require careful attention. In extraordinary cases, the Kaiser must have the right to place all or part of Belgium in a state of siege.

II.   *The Economic Penetration of Belgium*

Germany can only achieve a dominant economic influence over Belgium through the most extensive possible incorporation of this land into the German economic system.

1. This involves, first of all, taking Belgium into the German customs union. . . .

2. In the area of transport the most complete annexation possible is to be sought. . . .

3. The currency of Belgium is to be brought into conformity with that of the Reich. . . .

4. Beyond these measures, the protection of German industry against unfair competition from Belgium demands the greatest

possible equalization of conditions in the areas of social legislation and taxation. . . .

III.   Conclusion

The limitations on Belgian sovereignty which have been presented here as necessary are so grave that, according to those
psychological laws whose validity has been demonstrated
throughout history, they will imbue the Belgian Government
and the Belgian people with the inextinguishable yearning to
liberate themselves from them under any conditions and by every
means. The attempts of the Belgian Government, which are certainly to be expected, to free itself from its bonds by machinations with states hostile to us, as well as the equally certain more
or less dangerous movements of insurrection of the Belgian people would lead to the forceful intervention of the German occupation authorities, to the intervention of foreign powers, and
thus to a revision of Belgium's legal status.

4   FROM   *Petition of the Six Economic Associations, May 20, 1915*

*Bethmann Hollweg and his colleagues sought to censor public
discussion of war aims in order to preserve domestic harmony
and to help Germany's image abroad. As time passed, however,
it became impossible to silence the powerful groups and individuals supporting annexationism. The petition below is a good
illustration and classic expression of the kind of extremist position advocated by the most powerful economic and social groups
in the country.*

SOURCE (4). Reprinted from *Fall of the German Empire, 1914–1918*, Volume
I, pp. 312–320, edited by Ralph Haswell Lutz with the permission of the publishers, Stanford University Press. Copyright 1932 by the Board of Trustees
of the Leland Stanford Junior University.

The Agrarian League, the German Peasants League, the Christian German Peasants Unions, the Central Union of German Industrialists, the League of Industrialists, and the League of Middle-Class Citizens of the German Empire have on May 20, 1915, forwarded the following petition to the German Chancellor: . . . .

"EXCELLENCY!

"Together with the whole German people, those occupied in business pursuits, whether in agriculture or manufacture, in handicrafts or trade are determined to endure to the end, notwithstanding every sacrifice, in this struggle for life and death which has been forced upon Germany, in order that Germany may emerge stronger in its external relations, assured of a lasting peace, and thus also assured of further national, economic, and cultural development at home.

"Since the whole German people recognizes these aims as its own, and has given tangible proof of its willingness to make sacrifices for their achievement, the rumors recently circulating in town and country were bound to be most disquieting. These rumors (confirmed, apparently, by certain announcements in the press) were to the effect that preliminary steps were being taken to prepare the way for peace negotiations, and, in particular, for a separate peace with England, based on certain English wishes and demands.

"Hence universal satisfaction has been caused by the declaration of the *Norddeutsche Allgemeine Zeitung* that no competent judge would dream of sacrificing Germany's favorable military position in order to conclude a premature peace with any one of her enemies.

"Even if the military situation were more unfavorable, or more doubtful than it is, it should make no difference to our determination—unless, indeed, we are to lose sight of the aims in home and foreign policy which His Majesty the Emperor has himself proclaimed. These aims can be attained only by achieving a peace which will bring us better security for our frontiers in East and West, an extension of the foundations of our sea power, and the possibility of an unchecked and strong development of our economic resources; in short, those extensions of power, alike in politics, in the army, in the navy, and in our economic life, which will guarantee to us a stronger position in the world.

"Any peace which does not bring us these results will make a speedy renewal of the struggle inevitable under circumstances essentially less favorable to Germany. Therefore, no premature peace! For from a premature peace we could not hope for a sufficient prize of victory. Also no half-hearted peace, no peace which does not include complete political exploitation of those ultimate military successes which we expect to obtain!

"For it must be realized that the security of our future international position and our power to utilize the present self-sacrificing spirit of the German people for the settlement of those questions of domestic policy which will arise on the return of peace alike presuppose the complete exploitation of our military position for increasing Germany's power abroad. Assuredly our people would understand concessions wrung from them by a military situation so desperate as to oppose insuperable obstacles to any resistance however determined and self-sacrificing; but they would not tolerate concessions at the conclusion of peace not justified and necessitated by the military situation. Concessions of this kind would be fraught with the most fatal consequences for the domestic peace of our Fatherland, since they might lead to the same result as a premature withdrawal from the conflict, and our soldiers would discover, on returning home, that the only reward for their splendid endurance was a crushing burden of taxation. Hundreds of thousands have given their lives; the prize of victory must correspond to the sacrifice.

"The following memorandum was drawn up on March 10 of this year and addressed to Your Excellency by the Agrarian League, the German Peasants League, the Central Union of German Industrialists, the Industrialists League, and the League of Middle-Class Citizens in the German Empire. The memorandum, to which the Christian German Peasants Unions, who are also signatories to the present Petition, have given their adhesion, explains in detail the requirements which, the necessary military successes being assumed, must in the opinion of the undersigned associations be fulfilled in order to secure for Germany that political, military, and economic position which would enable her to look forward with confidence to the possibilities of the future. The memorandum was as follows:

'The undersigned corporations have carefully considered what measures are required to give effect to the formula which has so often been heard during the last few months, viz., that this war must be followed by an honorable peace corresponding to the sacrifices which have been made and containing in itself a guaranty for its continuance.

'In answering this question, it must never be forgotten that our enemies continue to announce that Germany is to be annihilated and struck out of the ranks of the Great Powers. Against such aims treaties will afford us no protection; for treaties, when the proper moment comes, would once more be trodden under foot. We can look for safety only in a serious economic and military weakening of our enemies sufficient to insure peace for as long a time as can be foreseen.

'We must demand a colonial empire adequate to satisfy Germany's manifold economic interests; we must safeguard our future policy in matters of customs and commerce; and we must secure a war indemnity to be paid in a form suitable to our requirements! But our chief aim in the struggle which has been forced upon us is, in our opinion, to strengthen and improve the foundations on which Germany's position in Europe rests, in the following directions:

'To provide the necessary security for our influence at sea and to secure our future military and economic position as against England. Belgium, owing to the close connection of Belgian territory (which is economically of such importance) with our main manufacturing districts, must be subjected to German Imperial legislation, in both military and tariff matters and also in regard to currency, banking, and postal arrangements. Her railways and canals must be incorporated in our transport system. In general, the government and administration of the country must be so managed that the inhabitants shall exert no influence on the political fortunes of the German Empire; there must be separation of the Walloon and of the predominantly Flemish territory; and all economic and industrial undertakings and real estate, which are so vital to the government of the country, must be transferred to German hands. We must consider the question of French territory from the same point of view; that is to say, the extent to which it affects our position toward England. Hence we must regard it as a matter of vital importance, in the interests of our future influence at sea, that we should hold the French coastal districts from the Belgian frontier approximately as far as the Somme, and thus secure access to the Atlantic Ocean. The Hinterland, which must be acquired with them, must be so delimited as to secure to us the complete economic and strategic exploitation of those Channel ports which we gain. Any further acquisitions of French territory, apart from the necessary annexation of the iron-ore district of Briey, must be determined solely by military and strategic considerations. After the experiences of this war, it may be regarded as self-evident that we cannot in the future leave our frontiers at the mercy of hostile invasion by allowing our opponents to retain those fortified positions which threaten us, in particular Verdun and Belfort and the Western slopes of the Vosges which lie between them. The acquisition of the line of the Meuse and the French Channel coast would carry with it possession not only of the iron-ore district of Briey mentioned above but also of the coal country in the departments of the Nord and Pas-de-Calais. These annexations also, as is self-evident after our experiences in Alsace-Lorraine, must be so arranged that the population of the annexed districts shall be precluded from exercising political influence on the fortunes of the German Empire; and all the economic resources of these districts, including both large and medium-sized estates, must be transferred to German hands on such terms that France shall compensate and retain their owners. As to the East, the determining consideration must be that the great addition to our manufacturing resources which we anticipate in the West must be counterbalanced by an equivalent annexation of agricultural territory in the East. The present economic structure of Germany has shown itself so fortunate in this war that it is hardly too much to say that every German is convinced of the necessity for maintaining it for as long a time as we can foresee.

'The necessity of strengthening the sound agricultural basis of our economic system, of making possible a German agricultural colonization on a large scale, of restoring the German peasants who are living abroad—especially those settled in Russia and at present deprived of their rights—to the territory of the Empire, so that they may take part in the economic life of Germany, and, lastly, of greatly increasing the numbers of our population capable of bearing arms implies a considerable extension of the

Imperial and Prussian frontiers in the East by annexation of at least parts of the Baltic Provinces and of those territories which lie to the south of them, while at the same time we must keep in mind the object of making our eastern German frontier capable of military defense. The restoration of East Prussia requires a better safeguarding of its frontiers by placing in front of them other districts; nor must West Prussia, Posen, and Silesia remain frontier marches exposed to danger as they now are.

'With regard to the granting of political rights to the inhabitants of the new districts and the safeguarding of German economic influence, what has already been said about France applies also. The war indemnity to be paid by Russia will have to consist to a large extent of the cession of land. Of course these demands depend on the hypothesis that military results will enable them to be carried out. But in view of what we have already achieved we confidently rely on our army and its leaders to gain a victory which will guarantee the attainment of these ends. We must pursue these ends not from a policy of conquest but because it is only by attaining them that we can secure that lasting peace which all classes of German people want in return for their sacrifices. Moreover, in our opinion, a voluntary surrender of hostile territories, in which so much German blood has been spilled and so many of our best and noblest have found a grave, would do violence to the sentiments of our people and to their conception of an honorable peace. In the future, as in the past, the want of harbors directly on the Channel would strangle our activity beyond the seas. An independent Belgium would continue to be a *tête de pont* to England, a point from which to attack us. If the natural line of fortifications of France were left in the hands of the French, there would be a permanent menace to our frontier; and Russia, if she emerged from the war without loss of territory, would underestimate our ability and power to prevent her doing injury to our interests, while, on the other hand, failure to win new agricultural territories on our eastern frontier would diminish the possibility of strengthening the defensive power of Germany against Russia by a sufficient increase of the German population.'

"We have the honor to draw Your Excellency's attention to the views expressed above, which are not confined to the undersigned associations but are widely held, possibly with occasional variations in detail, in many German circles which have not as yet publicly expressed them, and at the same time to inform you that we have simultaneously communicated this petition to the Ministries of the various Federated States.

"As a supplement to this memorandum, we must here lay stress on the fact that the political, military, and economic objects which the German people must strive after in the interests of the security of their future are inseparably connected with one another. It is clear, to start with, that the attainment of our great political objects depends on the offensive power and the successes of our army. But our actual experiences in this war prove, beyond any doubt, that our military successes, particularly in a long war, and their further exploitation depend to a large extent upon the economic strength and ability of our people. If German agriculture had not been in a position to secure the food of the people despite all the efforts of our enemies, and if German manufacturers, German inventive genius, and German technical skill had not been able to render us independent of foreign countries in the most different spheres, then, notwithstanding the brilliant successes of our victorious troops, we should have had to give way eventually in the struggle which has been forced upon us, if indeed we should not have been defeated already.

"Hence it follows that even those demands which seem at first sight to possess a purely economic significance must be viewed in the light of the urgent necessity for the greatest possible increase of our national strength, and also from a military standpoint."

• • •

5 FROM   *Resolutions of the Social*
              Democratic Party, August 11, 1916

*One of the consequences of the unrestrained annexationism of
right wing groups was the breakdown of the* Burgfrieden *during
1916. Food shortages, other wartime privations, and war weariness increased dissatisfaction among the workers. The Social
Democratic party, whose willingness to support the war effort
had been severely criticized by left wing elements in the party,
responded to this pressure from below by demanding domestic
reforms and a peace of understanding.*

COMRADES!

Two fatal years are behind us. Millions of sturdy human lives
have been destroyed; many hopes have failed; and countless
achievements of civilization have been ruined. Is this struggle that
devastates countries and annihilates peoples—the worst calamity
that has ever befallen civilized humanity—to continue still
longer? . . . .

The will for peace, which is as strong among the people of
enemy countries as in Germany, will undoubtedly be weakened
and set back when, like the chauvinistic annexationists in the
countries of the Entente, influential German circles set forth war
aims and propagate plans of conquest which will incite the people of those countries to the strongest resistance.

It seems to be the right time for the German people to take
a free and unhampered position in regard to these plans of conquest the realization of which would furnish the seeds of new
wars and which are more than likely to prolong the war.

The repeal of martial law demanded for a long time by the
Social-Democratic Party has not yet been secured. Besides, the

SOURCE (5). Reprinted from *Fall of the German Empire, 1914–1918*, Volume
I, p. 347, edited by Ralph Haswell Lutz with the permission of the publishers,
Stanford University Press. Copyright 1932 by the Board of Trustees of the
Leland Stanford Junior University.

permission to discuss war aims has not yet been granted. In spite of all that, desires of certain circles for annexation have again and again been made public and have been used to create a feeling in the enemy's countries.

On August 1 there took place in numerous German cities meetings of the "National Committees for a Victorious and Honorable Peace" in which most of the speakers discussed problems connected with war aims, probably in an annexationistic manner. After this, it is the clear duty of the Government to allow the general discussion of war aims. We have, therefore, in a memorial to the Chancellor, again demanded permission to discuss war aims.

We ask the party organizations to hold public meetings during the next few weeks in which they will take their stand on war and peace aims. We also request that preparations be made for the signing of a petition in which there is demanded a peace which will make friendship of neighboring peoples possible and which will secure territorial integrity, independence, and freedom of economic development for our country.

COMMITTEE OF THE SOCIAL-DEMOCRATIC
PARTY IN GERMANY

Berlin, August 11, 1916

THE GERMAN PEACE PROPOSAL
OF DECEMBER 12, 1916

At the close of 1916 the German government decided to issue a peace proposal inviting its enemies, through the good offices of the President of the United States, to enter into peace negotiations. Bethmann had been planning a German peace offensive for some time, but the sincerity of the December 12 action is subject to serious question. Although Bethmann had been encouraging President Wilson to mediate for several months, the German peace move was timed to precede anticipated American action and exclude America from participation in peace negotiations. The offer itself was too defiant in tone and too vague in content to receive anything but contemptuous rejection by Germany's enemies. It is possible that the actual offer did not reflect Bethmann's original intentions. By December 1916 Hindenburg and Ludendorff were in a position to block any moderation of Germany's war aims and the German Foreign Office had come under the direction of a hard liner, Arthur Zimmermann. Bethmann was not permitted to make the peace offer until it was absolutely clear that Germany was negotiating from a position of strength rather than weakness. Germany's smashing victory over Rumania and the German parliament's (Reichstag) passage of the Auxiliary Service Law mobilizing the civilian population for the war effort made the Supreme Command willing to allow Bethmann's offer. At the same time, the limits of Bethmann's flexibility in negotiation had been fairly well circumscribed. The Supreme Command had compelled the German government to establish a separate Kingdom of Poland which included the Russian portions of that divided country in early November. This action precluded a separate peace with Russia based on anything other than force. Furthermore, the anticipated peace move re-

quired negotiations between Berlin and Vienna concerning their respective war aims, and the German war aims, drawn up by Bethmann in consultation with the Supreme Command and with the approval of the Kaiser, could hardly prove attractive to the Allies (Document 6). Thus, there was good reason for the German note's vagueness (Document 7). Following the Allied rejection of the peace offer, the government felt it was in a position to call on the German people to renew their efforts (Document 8), and the Supreme Command felt justified in compelling Bethmann Hollweg to introduce unrestricted submarine warfare.

---

6   FROM   *Bethmann Hollweg to the German Ambassador in Vienna, Count Wedel*

Berlin, November 23, 1916

TELEGRAM NO. 460

Enclosed Your Excellency will find for your strictly confidential information . . . a presentation of our war aims. . . .

1.   Recognition of the Kingdom of Poland.

2.   Separation of Courland and Lithuanian territory (from Russia) and establishment of total border of German and Polish territory against Russia according to strategic considerations.

3.   French return of the occupied parts of Upper Alsace.

4.   Return of the French territory occupied by us with the proviso of strategic and economic border rectifications and extensions as well as a war indemnity.

5.   Restoration of Belgium as a sovereign state with definite guarantees for Germany, which are to be determined in negotiations with the King of the Belgians. In case these guarantees cannot be attained, annexation of Liège and adjacent areas.

6.   Luxemburg's entry into the German Empire as an independent federal state.

SOURCE (6). *Ursachen,* 2. Unterausschuss, Beilagen, Teil II, pp. 88–89.

7. Reestablishment of a German colonial empire in its previous extent and value by means of a general understanding in colonial matters (Belgian Congo).

8. Internationalization of Tsingtau.

9. Restoration of the territorial integrity of Greece if it remains neutral. Border rectification in northern Epirus as planned in case of neutrality.

10. Economic and financial adjustment to be made with consideration for the value of the territories conquered by both sides which are to be restored in the peace treaty.

11. Indemnification of German enterprises and private persons damaged by enemy measures of a non-military nature.

12. Renunciation of all economic agreements and measures which could constitute a barrier to the restoration of normal trade and commerce among all nations with conclusion of the appropriate trade treaties.

13. Freedom of the seas.

14. Restoration of free commerce on the lower Danube.

7 FROM   *The Peace Proposal,*
                December 12, 1916

MR. CHARGÉ D'AFFAIRES:

The most formidable war known to history has been ravaging for two and a half years a great part of the world. That catastrophe, that the bonds of a common civilization more than a thousand years old could not stop, strikes mankind in its most precious patrimony; it threatens to bury under its ruins the moral and physical progress on which Europe prided itself at the dawn of the 20th century. In that strife Germany and her allies, Austria-Hungary, Bulgaria, and Turkey, have given proof of their indestructi-

SOURCE (7). Reprinted from *Fall of the German Empire, 1914–1918,* Volume I, pp. 398–399, edited by Ralph Haswell Lutz with the permission of the publishers, Stanford University Press. Copyright 1932 by the Board of Trustees of the Leland Stanford Junior University.

ble strength in winning considerable successes at war. Their unshakable lines resist ceaseless attacks of their enemies' arms. The recent diversion in the Balkans was speedily and victoriously thwarted. The latest events have demonstrated that a continuation of the war cannot break their resisting power. The general situation much rather justifies their hope of fresh successes. It was for the defense of their existence and freedom of their national development that the four allied powers were constrained to take up arms. The exploits of their armies have brought no change therein. Not for an instant have they swerved from the conviction that the respect of the rights of other nations is not in any degree incompatible with their own rights and legitimate interests. They do not seek to crush or annihilate their adversaries. Conscious of their military and economic strength and ready to carry on to the end, if they must, the struggle that is forced upon them, but animated at the same time by the desire to stem the flood of blood and to bring the horrors of war to an end, the four allied powers propose to enter even now into peace negotiations. They feel sure that the propositions which they would bring forward, and which would aim to assure the existence, honor, and free development of their peoples, would be such as to serve as a basis for the restoration of a lasting peace.

If, notwithstanding this offer of peace and conciliation, the struggle should continue, the four allied powers are resolved to carry it on to a victorious end, while solemnly disclaiming any responsibility before mankind and history.

The Imperial Government has the honor to ask through your obliging medium the Government of the United States to be pleased to transmit the present communication to the Government of the French Republic, to the Royal Government of Great Britain, to the Imperial Government of Japan, to the Royal Government of Rumania, to the Imperial Government of Russia, and to the Royal Government of Serbia.

I take this opportunity to renew to you, Mr. Chargé d'Affaires, the assurance of my high consideration.

VON BETHMANN-HOLLWEG

To Mr. Joseph Clark Grew,
Chargé d'Affaires of the
United States of America   Grew

8 *To My Army and My Navy*

In unison with the rulers allied to me I proposed to our enemies to enter into immediate peace negotiations. The enemies have declined my offer. Their lust for power contemplates the destruction of Germany.

The war goes on!

The heavy responsibility before God and men for all the future terrible sacrifices, which my desire wished to spare you, falls upon the enemy governments.

In righteous indignation over the enemy's insolence and in the desire to defend our most sacred possessions and to secure for the Fatherland a happy future, you must harden into steel.

Our enemies did not want the conciliation which I offered them. With God's help our weapons shall force them to it.

WILHELM I. R.

GREAT HEADQUARTERS, January 5, 1917

SOURCE (8). Reprinted from *Fall of the German Empire, 1914–1918*, Volume I, p. 400, edited by Ralph Haswell Lutz with the permission of the publishers, Stanford University Press. Copyright 1932 by the Board of Trustees of the Leland Stanford Junior University.

THE KREUZNACH DISCUSSIONS,
APRIL 23, 1917

Although the German peace offer of December 12, 1916 had compelled Bethmann to set up a list of war aims to be discussed in the proposed peace negotiations, the rejection of the peace offer momentarily terminated the fixing of a specific war aims program. This situation proved satisfactory neither to the German Supreme Command nor to the Austro-Hungarian Foreign Minister, Count Ottokar Czernin. Ludendorff distrusted Bethmann and wanted a fixed minimum program of war aims. Czernin felt that Austria-Hungary was on its last legs and could only be saved by a negotiated peace based on a moderate war aims program. These combined pressures, exerted for such different reasons, led to the formulation of the Kreuznach Program (Document 9). This program demonstrates Ludendorff's domination of German foreign policy and Germany's dominant position in the Dual Alliance. How committed, however, was Bethmann to the Kreuznach Program? Some historians have argued that his signature on the Kreuznach Program demonstrates that he was in substantial agreement with its terms, while others have stressed the reservations contained in a minute he placed in the files on May 1, 1917 (Document 10). His speech to the Reichstag on May 15, 1917 (Document 11) mirrors the ambiguity of the then secret documents.

---

9   FROM   *Record of the Kreuznach*
                  Discussions

Final Draft
April 23, 1917

THE EAST

1. Courland and Lithuania are to be won for the German Empire. . . . Should it be possible to acquire parts of the other Baltic provinces . . . then the effort should be made. . . .

2. The formation of the German-Polish border is dependent on the future relationship between Poland and the German Empire, concerning which an understanding must now be made with Austria-Hungary. If we succeed in securing our military, political and economic predominance in Poland, then the Supreme Command can relent on the boundary line previously demanded. In any case, the Narev Line, and further the line Ostrolenka-Mlawa, a buffer for Thorn, the corner north of Kalisch, and a buffer zone for the Upper Silesian industrial region remain necessary. An effort is to be made to arrange the Germanization of the border strip at the peace negotiations.

In establishing the Polish eastern border one may consider giving the Polish state the possibility of expanding in the East. However, the agreement concerning Courland and Lithuania is not to be endangered by this.

3. Russia may be compensated for the loss of Courland and Lithuania in East Galicia . . . and on the Moldau. . . .

In Western Walachia, Austria-Hungary needs the area up to Craiova in order to keep Rumania militarily in hand. Insofar as the areas have not already been granted to Bulgaria, Serbia with Montenegro and Albania can be joined to Austria-Hungary as a South Slavic state.

Bulgaria should only receive limited territory in the Dobrudja beyond the 1913 border. In any case, the connection Cernavoda-Constanza must remain Rumanian because of our interests in Turkey.

SOURCE (9). *Ursachen*, 2. Unterausschuss, Beilagen, Teil II, pp. 200–202.

The securing of German oil interests in Rumania must be achieved.

THE WEST

1. Belgium continues to exist and remains in German military control until it is politically and economically ready for a defensive and offensive alliance with Germany. Germany is to determine the end of this period of transition. However, for military-strategic reasons Liège and the Flemish coast along with Bruges are to remain permanently (or in 99 year lease) in German hands. These separations are non-negotiable conditions for peace with England. . . .

2. The separation of the southeast corner of Belgium (Arlon area) is demanded by the Supreme Command for military-economic reasons on the assumption that it contains ore. . . .

3. The ore and coal district of Briey-Longwy must be won for Germany. In other parts of the *Reichsland* (Alsace-Lorraine) there are to be small border rectifications for military reasons. . . .

4. In the most extreme case, France may receive a few corners of the border and a narrow border strip southwest of Mühlhausen in order not to let a peace with France fail. But in no case are there to be German losses in the Vosges valleys.

His Majesty the Emperor suggests that France should be compensated for the French territories she is losing to Germany with the Belgian corner of Mariembourg (southwest Givet). . . .

GENERAL

An armistice is to be limited to the war on land; the war at sea continues.

The further questions of the Balkans and Asia Minor, the question of the naval bases demanded in the memorandum of the Admiralty, as well as the question of colonies still have to be settled by the agencies involved.

Bethmann Hollweg	von Hindenburg
Zimmermann	Ludendorff
von Hoetzendorff	

10   *Written Statement by Bethmann Hollweg for the Record, May 1, 1917*

General Ludendorff has been pressing for an agreement on war aims for some time and has also managed to suggest to His Majesty that this is the most important item of business at the present time. Since military operations do not depend on this and since at the moment there is no possibility for peace negotiations, there must be some hidden intention behind this. Probably the general hopes to bring about my downfall through differences of opinion on war aims, something that would probably be easy to accomplish at the present moment. Or he believes that he can pin me down, so that I will not conduct peace negotiations on a cheaper basis (Peace offer of December 12). I have co-signed the protocol because it would be laughable to depart over phantasies. Naturally, I will in no way allow myself to be bound by the protocol. If possibilities of peace open up anywhere and by any means, I will pursue them. I wish to have this formally stated for the record here.

SOURCE (10). Translated by the editor from Kuno Graf von Westarp, *Konservative Politik im letzten Jahrzehnt des Kaiserreiches,* Vol. II, pp. 85–86 (Berlin, Deutsche Verlagsanstalt, 1935).

11 FROM   *Address of the Imperial Chancellor to the Reichstag, May 15, 1917*

Gentlemen, the interpellations which have just now been brought forward demand from me a definite, detailed statement regarding the question of our war aims. To make such a state-

SOURCE (11). Reprinted from *Fall of the German Empire, 1914–1918,* Volume I, pp. 354–358, edited by Ralph Haswell Lutz with the permission of the publishers, Stanford University Press. Copyright 1932 by the Board of Trustees of the Leland Stanford Junior University.

ment at the present moment would not serve the interests of the country. ["*Quite right!*"—*Left.*] I must, therefore, decline to make one. [*Applause from the Left.*]

Since the winter of 1914–15 I have been pressed first on one side and then on another to make a public statement of our war aims, if possible with details. [*Shouts from the Right of "Not Details!"*] They are being demanded of me every day, Herr Roesicke. [*Denials from the Right.*] To force me to speak, various parties and tendencies have interpreted my silence on declarations of war aims, as giving my assent to their programs. When giving permission for a free discussion concerning our war aims, I expressly declared that the Government could not and would not take part in any controversy. I protested against any positive conclusions whatever as to the Government's attitude being drawn from the Government's silence. ["*Hear, hear!*"—*Right.*] I now repeat this protest in the most emphatic manner. ["*Bravo!*" —*Left and Center.*]

What I was able to say at any time about our war aims I have said here publicly in the Reichstag. They were fundamental principles—they could not be more than that [cheers]—but they were sufficiently clear to exclude identification with other programs which have been made public. [*Approval.*] I have adhered to these fundamental principles until now. They also found solemn expression in the peace offer made conjointly with our allies on December 12, 1916. [*Cheers.*] The supposition which has recently arisen that some differences of opinion existed between us and our allies regarding the question of peace belongs to the realm of fable. [*Loud cheers by the German "Fraktion," Center, National-Liberals, and Left.*] I expressly state this now with the conviction that I am also expressing the opinion of the leading statesmen of the powers allied to us. [*Renewed applause.*]

Gentlemen, I thoroughly and completely understand the passionate interest of the people in our war aims and the conditions of peace. I understand the demand for a precise statement which was addressed to me today from the Right and the Left. But in a debate on war aims the only guiding line for me is an early and satisfactory conclusion of the war. [*Loud cheers.*] Beyond that I cannot do anything. If the general situation obliges me to maintain an attitude of reserve, as is the case at present, I will maintain this reserve, and no pressure from either Herr Scheidemann or Herr Roesicke will force me to depart from my path. [*Cries on the Left, "Roesicke began it," and laughter.*]

I will not allow myself to be led astray by the speech with which Herr Scheidemann, at a time when the drumfire is being heard on the Aisne and at Arras, believed he could disseminate among the people the possibility of a revolution. [*Stormy applause from Right, Center, and Left.*]

Gentlemen, the German people, like myself, will fail to understand this speech. But just as little will I allow myself to be diverted from my course by Herr Roesicke's attempt to represent me as treading the paths of Social-Democracy. I will not allow myself to be forced into the paths of either party [*hearty applause by National-Liberals, Center, Progressive People's Party, and German "Fraktion"*], either by the Left, or by you [*turning to the Conservatives.*] No, gentlemen, certainly not; my paths are entirely those of the German nation, whom alone I have to serve, whose sons, one and all, are fighting for the life and being of the nation, standing firm about their Kaiser, whom they trust and who trusts them. [*Applause.*] Gentlemen, the Kaiser's words of August will live on; they have not been falsified nor proved falsely stamped by the course of time. Herr Roesicke, who has here put on airs as the special guardian of those words [*"Very good!"—Left*] will be able to read the necessary answer to his question whether the Kaiser's word still holds good in the Kaiser's Easter message, countersigned by me. [*"Quite right!"—Left.*]

I trust that the reserve which I must exercise—and it would be unscrupulousness on my part if I failed to exercise it—will find the support of the majority of the Reichstag and also of the people. [*Approval by Center, National-Liberals, Progressive People's Party.*] For the past month unparalleled battles have been raging on the Western front. The whole people, with all its feelings and anxieties, its thought and its thanks, is present with its sons out there, who, with unexampled tenacity and contempt of death, are resisting the attacks daily renewed by the British and the French. [*Loud cheers.*]

Even today I see no readiness for peace on the part of Great Britain and France and no abandonment of their excessive aims of conquest or economic destruction. Who, then, were the strong ones whose governments openly stood up last winter before the world in order to bring this insane slaughter of nations to a conclusion? Were they in London or Paris? The most recent declarations which I have seen from London state that the war aims which were announced two years ago remain unaltered.

Even Herr Scheidemann does not believe that I could answer this declaration with a *beau geste.* Does anyone believe, in view of the state of mind of our Western enemies, that they could be induced to conclude peace by a program of renunciation? [*"Very true!"*] It comes to this: Shall I immediately give our enemies an assurance which would enable them to prolong the war indefinitely without danger of losses to themselves? Shall I inform these enemies that, come what may, we shall under any circumstances be the people which renounce—we shall not touch a hair of your heads; but you, who want our lives, may without any risk continue to try your luck? Shall I nail down the German Empire in all directions by a one-sided statement which comprises only one part of the total peace conditions, renounces the successes gained by the blood of our sons and brothers, and leaves everything else in a state of suspension? [*"Quite right!"*] No! I reject such a policy. [*Prolonged cheers.*] I will not pursue a policy which would be the basest ingratitude toward the heroic deeds of our people before Arras and on the Aisne. It would permanently weigh down our people, to the humblest worker, in all conditions of life, and would be equivalent to surrendering the future of our Fatherland.

On the other hand, perhaps I ought to lay down a program of conquest? I decline to do that also. [*Cries on the Right: "Why do you say that to us?" Laughter on the Left.*] If it has not been demanded, then we are of one opinion. I say again, I also decline to lay down a program of conquest. We did not go to war, and we are not fighting now against almost the whole world, in order to make conquests, but only to secure our existence and firmly to establish the future of the nation. A program of conquest is as little helpful in achieving victory and ending the war as a program of renunciation. On the contrary, in doing so I should only be playing the game of the hostile rulers and making it easier for them further to dupe their war-weary peoples into an immeasurable prolongation of the war. That also would be base ingratitude toward our warriors before Arras and on the Aisne.

As regards our Eastern neighbor, Russia, I have already spoken recently. It seems as if new Russia has renounced her violent

plans of conquest. Whether or not Russia will act or can influence
her allies in the same direction I am unable to estimate. Doubt-
less Great Britain, with the assistance of her other allies, is doing
her utmost to keep Russia in the future also harnessed to Britain's
war chariot [*loud cries of "Hear, hear!"*] and to oppose Russian
wishes for the speedy restoration of world peace. If, however,
Russia desires to prevent further bloodshed of her sons and renounces for herself all violent plans of conquest, if she wishes
to restore the permanent relations of peaceful life side by side
with us, then it surely results as a matter of course that we, since
we share this desire, will not prevent the establishment of permanent relations in the future, and will not render their development impossible by demands [*loud and prolonged cheers*] which
would not be in accordance with the ideal of the freedom of
nations and would lay the germ of enmity in the Russian nation.
I do not doubt that an agreement aiming exclusively at a mutual
understanding could be obtained which would exclude every
thought of oppression and leave behind no sting of discord.
[*Loud cheers.*]

Our military position has never been so good since the beginning of the war. [*Cheers.*] The enemy in the West, in spite of
their most terrible losses, cannot break through. Our U-boats
are operating with increasing success. [*Cheers.*] I will not employ
any fine words about them. The deeds of our U-boat men speak
for themselves. [*Loud applause.*] I think that even the neutrals
will recognize this. As far as is compatible with our duty toward
our own people, who come first, we take into account the interests
of the neutral states. The concessions which we made to them
are not empty promises. That is so in regard to our neighbors
on the frontier, Holland and Scandinavia, as well as those states
which, because of their geographical position, are greatly exposed
to enemy pressure. I am thinking in this connection especially of
Spain, which, in loyalty to her noble traditions, is endeavoring
under great difficulties to preserve her independent policy of
neutrality. We thankfully recognize this attitude, and have only
one wish, namely, that the Spanish people may reap the reward
of their strong independent policy by a development of their
power and further prosperity. [*Loud applause.*]

Thus time is on our side. In full confidence we can trust that
we are approaching a satisfactory conclusion. Then the time will

come when we can negotiate with our enemies about our war aims, regarding which I am in full harmony with the Supreme Army Command. [*Loud cheers.*] Then we shall attain a peace which will bring us liberty to rebuild what the war has destroyed in unimpaired development of our strength, so that from all the blood and all the sacrifices an empire, a people, will rise again strong, independent, unthreatened by its enemies, a bulwark of peace and labor. [*Prolonged cheers.*]

THE REICHSTAG PEACE
RESOLUTION

12   *The Reichstag Peace*
            Resolution of July 19, 1917

Bethmann's policy of the "diagonal," his attempt to pacify the left with promises of domestic reform and the right with intimations of an annexationist peace, finally collapsed in July 1917. When unrestricted submarine warfare failed to bring England to her knees in six months as the navy had promised, the Catholic Center party leader, Matthias Erzberger, exposed the navy's miscalculations and called on the Reichstag to take a more active role in foreign affairs and pass a resolution calling for a peace of understanding. The proposed peace resolution was opposed by the Supreme Command and by Bethmann Hollweg. Bethmann, however, earned the enmity of both sides. The generals accused him of letting the domestic situation get out of hand, and the Reichstag parties who had previously supported him now expressed their loss of confidence in him or remained passive while the Supreme Command forced the Kaiser to dismiss the Chancellor. The Supreme Command, however, was unable to prevent the passage of the peace resolution (Document 12). Some historians have pointed out that the wording of the peace resolution was too vague to be meaningful. In any case, whatever impression it might have made was largely vitiated when the

SOURCE (12). Reprinted from *Fall of the German Empire, 1914–1918*, Volume II, pp. 282–283, edited by Ralph Haswell Lutz with the permission of the publishers, Stanford University Press. Copyright 1932 by the Board of Trustees of the Leland Stanford Junior University.

*new Chancellor, Georg Michaelis, accepted the Resolution "as
I understand it." The effect of Bethmann's departure left the
situation as unclear as it had been while he was in office, and
Bethmann's attempts to explain his policy in his postwar memoirs
(Document 13) provided the image of the wartime Chancellor
that was to dominate the historical literature until the revelations
of Professor Fischer.*

The Reichstag strives for a peace of understanding and the
permanent reconciliation of peoples. Forced territorial acquisitions and political, economic, or financial oppressions are ir-
reconcilable with such a peace. The Reichstag also rejects all
plans which aim at economic isolation and hostility among nations after the war. The freedom of the seas must be made secure.
Only an economic peace will prepare the ground for a friendly
intercourse between the nations. The Reichstag will strongly
promote the creation of international judicial organizations.
However, as long as the enemy governments will not enter upon
such a peace, as long as they threaten Germany and her allies with
conquests and coercion, the German nation will stand together
as a man and steadfastly hold out and fight until its own and its
allies' right to life and development is secured. The German
nation is invincible in its unity. The Reichstag knows that in
this respect it is in harmony with the men who in heroic struggle
are defending the Fatherland. The imperishable gratitude of the
whole people is assured them.

13   FROM   *Bethmann Hollweg*
          Observations on the World War

The difficulty of the monumental task which the war presented
to us was at first underestimated by the people. The confidence
in our military superiority was practically without limit. This
unconditional certainty of victory, which was not dissipated even
by the outcome of the Battle of the Marne and—despite splendid
victories—the completely undecided situation in the East, was,
leaving aside all the self-deception it harboured, a moral factor
of enormous importance. It is easy to make the *post facto* criticism which ascribes the excess of this confidence to the inadequate
informing of the public about the true state of affairs. Who can
now decide if the nation's capacity for resistance against the
overwhelming strength of the world would have remained intact
so splendidly and so long if the Supreme Command had una-
bashedly announced in September 1914 that our war plan had
failed with the Battle of the Marne? How would such a disen-
chantment have affected our Austrian ally, who was even more
hard-pressed than ourselves? Who would then maintain that it
would still have remained possible to have at least delayed Italy's
decision and to have gained allies such as those we found in Turkey and Bulgaria? The damage was caused, not by the mood of
victory, but rather by its misuse for the untimely elaboration of
excessive war aims. And certainly the intellectual circles, who
drove the people into the war aims movement, could have recognized even without an overt indication that at the very least no
dictated peace was in the offing. By means of the London Agreement England had secured herself against any separate peace on
the part of her allies. Italy, as all the world could recognize, was
pursuing a connection with the Entente. The return of the
French Government from Bordeaux to Paris underlined the results of the Battle of the Marne. The flower of Germany's youth
bled before Ypres. And while the western front bogged down in
the trenches, the Russian danger grew continuously. Nothing

SOURCE (13). Translated by the editor from Th. von Bethmann Hollweg,
Betrachtungen zum Weltkriege, Vol. II, pp. 25–31 (Berlin, Verlag Reimar
Hobbing, 1921). Reprinted by permission of the publisher.

would have been lost if one kept quiet about war aims. If there were possibilities of peace in the first months of 1915—personally, I doubt them—then certainly they were at best for a peace based on the *status quo ante,* that is, precisely for the opposite of the programs then being proposed.

Without a doubt there was at the beginning support for more extensive war aims among the entire people irrespective of political tendency. The victorious troops and a homefront confident of victory were certain that a much stronger Germany should emerge from the war. The idea that the complete surrender of the territory conquered at the cost of so much blood would be a violation of our obligation to the fallen also developed out of the general emotional atmosphere. Aspirations with regard to Belgium were particularly popular because of the hatred of England. A correct instinctive feeling recognized that the war as well as its outbreak had only become possible because of England's policy and that its course was determined by England. Seeking security against England in Belgium was so popular that it was stubbornly supported by a large Reichstag majority until the spring of 1917.

The attitude of broad segments of the population changed before this was expressed in the parliaments. No one believed that we could be completely defeated. But that, on the other hand, it would be we who would drive the enemy to submission was an idea which found no acceptance on the part of the common man because he drew sober and practical conclusions from the blockade and the numerical superiority of the enemy. When peace did not come closer despite the fact that we stood deep in enemy territory, when the enemy continually acquired new allies while with us everything became visibly scarcer, then simple common sense said that time was working against us. In the face of such sentiment, the conflict over war aims became increasingly incomprehensible. One wanted to win in order to end the war, but not in order to conquer territories. The (unrestricted) submarine warfare decision was so joyously greeted at the beginning of 1917, not because one hoped to get the Flemish coast, but because one hoped to win peace by it. For these reasons no one spoke of the instability caused by the wartime scarcities or of despair at the final outcome. The people gave their utmost in their boundless confidence that the war could not end badly

under the leadership of Hindenburg and Ludendorff. But even
when it was not going badly, they wanted to see it end.

According to my impressions, such views, developing gradually,
became more widespread and deeply felt after the winter of
1916–17 than the press and Reichstag wanted to have believed.
With the passage of time, they became the general attitude of
those circles who, to be sure, did not raise their voices publicly,
but behind whom their stood reality.

The natural result of my conception of the total situation was
that I tried to suppress the public debate over war aims insofar
as I was able. Neither annexationism nor the pacifist defeatism
provoked by its excesses made any easier the task dictated by
our military situation, namely, the promotion of an inclination
to peace on the part of the enemy. Only the promoters of the
war on the enemy side were strengthened. The enemy found
valuable allies in the German enthusiasts for conquests as well
as in those who called for renunciations.

It was false to believe that the establishment of further war
aims was likely to maintain our will to victory. If the masses,
without whom the war could not be conducted, were taken with
the idea that we had to do what was necessary to withstand the
enemy superiority, then further war aims created no enthusiasm
but rather insulted simple common sense. . . . Partisan agitation
in the course of the war easily brought the war aims of the annexationists under the suspicion of serving special interests among
the masses who suffered most from the wartime scarcities and
were thus most endangered by the war.

I also could not judge the sentiment in the army any other way.
The German army did not lack its confidence in victory, without
which no army can fight and win, until the end. In his feeling
of duty and patriotism, the German soldier performed almost
superhumanly because he so firmly trusted the leadership of
Hindenburg and Ludendorff. But never in the bloody seriousness
of the situation, which the troops experienced most directly,
could the idea arise that it did not pay to face the enemy fire
because afterward a weak peace would be concluded.[1] On the

---

[1] This claim, that is, that the troops would lose their morale if they thought
that all Germany was going to get was a *status quo* peace and, conversely,
that the troops would fight harder if they had concrete war aims to fight for,
was continually made by the Supreme Command. It is interesting and highly

contrary, at least from the winter of 1916–17 on, the concern that peace could be lost because of aims of conquest despite all their heroic deeds had a depressing effect. As in the homeland, so in the army, confidence in victory was independent of intentions of conquest.

The necessity of defence had brought the people together in a marvelous way at the outbreak of the war. If the unity became shaky, if the sons of the same people began to speak such different languages because of the phantom of war aims that no one understood the other, then complete disintegration could only be prevented if the nation found its way back to the spirit which had filled it in August 1914. There lay the only great idea which had the power of unifying. It was appropriate to the military situation and to the true will of the nation which, far from all Pan-German excesses, only sought to maintain the position in Europe and the world to which its industriousness had given it an indestructable right. My policy was designed to carry the people out of the exuberance of the first months back to the ground of reality. This could not be done abruptly if a division was not going to be promoted in which the will to fight and confidence were lost. . . . A development along these lines without crisis would have been possible if the proponents of increased war aims were not repeatedly strengthened in their views through the support which they received from the military leadership after August 1916.

revealing of the atmosphere in the Weimar Republic to note the extent to which Bethmann feels compelled to defend himself, not against those who accused him of supporting excessive war aims, but rather against critics on the right who attacked him for his weak leadership and wartime moderation.— G.D.F.

14 FROM   *Results of the War Aims*
             Discussion Between Michaelis and the
             Supreme Command, August 9, 1917

The Supreme Command found the promotion of annexationist war aims somewhat easier after the fall of Bethmann Hollweg. In a meeting with Michaelis on August 9, 1917 they committed the new Chancellor to an extensive war aims program and urged him to force this program on Germany's Austro-Hungarian ally. The chief, although by no means the only, source of contention between Germany and Austria-Hungary was Poland. Following the proclamation of an "independent" Poland in November 1916 the so-called "Austro-Polish" solution was favored. This solution, as the term implies, would have placed Poland under Austro-Hungarian domination through the establishment of a Kingdom of Poland ruled by a member of the House of Habsburg. In return, the Germans demanded a predominant position in the Polish economy and a large frontier strip in the area of the Nieman River to act as a buffer between Prussia's Polish provinces and the projected Austrian Poland. By the spring of 1917, however, the Germans were taking advantage of the weakness of their ally by calling for a German control over Poland, including Galicia, which had belonged to the Austro-Hungarian Empire during the war. In return, the Germans were willing to compensate the Austro-Hungarians in Rumania, although here, too, they were demanding economic predominance. Furthermore, the Germans were demanding that Austria-Hungary bind herself to Germany in a military and economic sense more closely than ever before. The Central Powers squabbled over these issues, the Germans becoming ever more demanding and the Austrians ever more procrastinating, until the end of the war.

SOURCE (14). Translated by the editor from *Ursachen*, 2. Unterausschuss, Beilagen, Teil II, pp. 204–206.

10. THE QUESTION OF
COURLAND AND LITHUANIA

The Reich Chancellor and the Supreme Command are agreed that the Duchy of Courland and the Grand Principality of Lithuania must be associated with Germany in a close relationship. The form of association remains temporarily undetermined. . . .

In answer to the question which has been raised, the Supreme Command declared an acceptance of the line of the Nieman River is not possible, not only for political (Folkish) but also for military reasons, and that giving Wilna to the Polish state is militarily impermissible.

The Supreme Command emphasized the importance of church influences for the development of Lithuania: The three bishoprics must be given to Lithuanians, and the Polish influence pushed aside by the separation of the Bishopric of Seiny from Warsaw.

Lithuania should not be germanized; the question of colonization requires the greatest caution.

11. BALTIC PROVINCES AND FINLAND

The English influence must be countered. Contact with the leading Balts and Finns is necessary to accomplish this.

The Supreme Command and the leadership of the Reich agree to combine their previously separate activity among the Balts and Finns.

12. THE UKRAINE

An effort should be made to get a clear picture of the (separatist) efforts in the Ukraine. The movement should be used to promote a secret friendly connection with us. An agreement must be made with Austria as to whether one can offer the Ukrainians part of East Galicia.

13.   POLAND

It is impossible for Germany to accept an Austrian Poland. We are bound to the proclamation of November 5, 1916. The connection of Poland with Germany is only possible if Austria disinterests herself in Poland and also renounces Lublin.

First step: Unification of the General Government, and installation of a Regent (Duke Albrecht).

If Austria does not agree to the unification of the Government, then the further development of the Polish state must be handled in a dilatory manner. . . .

If the Poles fail, then let a fourth partition of Poland take place.

The border rectifications must then be more extensive (entire Narev Line!) than had previously been intended under the assumption of a Poland dependent upon Germany (See the protocol of the discussions of April 23, 1917, East, No. 2).[1]

If nothing comes of the attachment of Poland to Germany, then the basis for our acceptance of Austrian predominance in Rumania collapses.

We have nothing to gain from an Austrian renunciation of Galicia at the present time.

14.   RUMANIA

The Kreuznach agreements regarding Rumania are to be maintained so long as the assumptions on which they are based (Courland-Lithuania, Poland) are not changed.

The Rumanian Dobrudja should not go to Bulgaria.

15.   BELGIUM

The Belgian question is the heart of the conflict with England. The Supreme Command repeats its demands because of military

[1] Reading number 9.

considerations (See the protocol of the discussions of April 23, 1917, West, No. 1).

Belgium must remain in our hands as a special state so that we can use the French-Belgian border as a base of operations with the Flemish coast as a cover against England. The Supreme Command recognizes that these demands can only be attained if England is forced to give in. If we cannot chain Belgium to us in this way, then we must at least have Liège with its northern perimeter to protect the industrial region around Aachen.

16. LUXEMBURG

The Luxemburg question should be brought up as little as possible so that the attachment of Luxemburg to Germany can be accomplished as quietly as possible. Luxemburg must not have a direct border with France. The Luxemburg railroad system must be joined to the Prusso-Hessian Railroad Association.

17. LONGWY-BRIEY

The "coal and ore district of Longwy-Briey" (with its northern extensions into Belgium) is economically indispensable for us.

Consideration for French feelings can be taken in the kind of political connection which is created.

An expansion of the fortress area around Metz toward the West, however, is desirable.

18. CENTRAL EUROPEAN ECONOMIC ALLIANCE

It was emphasized that economic and military agreements are of decisive importance for the continued maintenance of the present four power alliance in peacetime.

Michaelis   von Hindenburg

15   *Manifesto of the German*
      Vaterlands-Partei, September 12, 1917

The annexationist leaders, recognizing the need to mobilize popular support for their position and to counter Socialist agitation for a negotiated peace of understanding, founded the Vaterlands-Partei on the anniversary of the Battle of Sedan (1871). More a patriotic movement than an actual political party, the Vaterlands-Partei has often been called protofascist by historians. The Supreme Command probably inspired its founding, but the most important work was done by Grand Admiral Alfred von Tirpitz, who was largely responsible for the building of the German High Seas Fleet before the war, and Wolfgang Kapp, a Pan-German and government official in Prussia who was to lead an abortive putsch against the Weimar Republic in 1920. The party soon had a million and a half members, but it collapsed even more speedily than it had grown in October 1918. This suggests that the popularity of the movement largely was due to the Supreme Command's continuous promises of victory and misleadingly optimistic reports from the front.

Large sections of the German public are not in agreement with the attitude of the present Reichstag majority regarding the most vital questions of the Fatherland. They consider the endeavor to place conflict on constitutional questions in the foreground as a danger to the Fatherland and an advantage to the enemy, especially now, when the fate of the Empire is at stake. They do not consider that the Reichstag elected before the war really any longer represents the will of the German people. Who is there that does not long for peace with all his heart? *Nervous and weak peace manifestoes,* however, only postpone peace. Our enemies, bent on the destruction of Germany, see signs only of

SOURCE (15). Reprinted from *Fall of the German Empire, 1914–1918,* Volume I, pp. 368–370, edited by Ralph Haswell Lutz with the permission of the publishers, Stanford University Press. Copyright 1932 by the Board of Trustees of the Leland Stanford Junior University.

collapse in them. And this, too, at a time when, according to our Hindenburg, *our military situation is better than ever*. If we convince the enemy that he can have an honorable peace by negotiation at any moment, he will have nothing to gain and everything to lose by continuing the war. In the light of past events, our Government is in a dilemma. *Without strong support from the people the Government by itself cannot master the situation.* For a strong imperial policy it needs a strong instrument. Such an instrument must be provided in the form of a large party based on all sections of the Fatherland.

The German Empire should now be not split by party strife but united in the will to victory! Calling to mind with gratitude our first beloved Emperor of undying memory and his iron Chancellor, who united the German peoples, devoted to a titanic struggle against *destructive party strife,* against which Otto von Bismarck appealed before God and the people, the undersigned men of East Prussia, true to the traditions of their forebears, *have founded the*

German Vaterlands-Partei

to guard and shield the German Fatherland in this gravest hour of German history from the evil of disunion and division.

The German Vaterlands-Partei aims at welding together the whole energy of the Fatherland without distinction of party politics. It consists of patriotic individuals and associations. It will support and defend a strong Government which can reflect the signs of the times, not in weak concessions at home and abroad, but in a resolutely German and unshakable belief in victory.

The German Vaterlands-Partei will not enter into rivalry with patriotically minded political parties. *With these* it will work hand in hand for the confirmation of the will to conquer and to overcome difficulties. *The German Vaterlands-Partei* is a party of union. *It does not, therefore, contemplate setting up its own parliamentary candidates.* When peace is proclaimed it will dissolve. We want no internal strife. We Germans are apt too easily to forget the war in internal quarrels. Not for a moment does the enemy forget them! The Germans united in the German Vaterlands-Partei pledge themselves to do everything to preserve internal concord until the conclusion of peace. *However any individual may view vexed questions of internal politics, the decision of these is to be postponed till after the war.* Then our heroes will have returned from the battlefield and will be able to co-operate in the internal construction of the Empire. Now victory is all that matters!

We do not live, as our enemies falsely pretend, under autocratic absolutism, but surrounded by the blessings of a constitutional state whose social activities put to shame all the democracies of the world, and which has given the German nation the strength to defy the enormously superior power of the enemy. *German freedom stands heaven-high above the unreal democracies and all their vaunted blessings,* which English hypocrisy and Wilson prate of in order thereby to destroy Germany, which is impregnable against their weapons. We will not further England's interests.

We know, and all the Germans in the world know, that it is not for Germans, as for the English, a matter of business! *England, the originator of the world conflagration, is in a critical position. We are victorious on land and on sea!* Hit in her most vital spot by the submarine campaign, England is placing her last hopes on German unrest and disunion. The time is not far off when her pride will be humbled, if we can only endure and withstand deceitful peace-kites!

We know, and the enemy knows too, how much Germany has to thank the Kings of Prussia of the House of Hohenzollern for her military education. In the existence of the Emperor the enemy sees the chief obstacle to the defeat of Germany. By means of cunning and lies they want to encourage Germany's sons to *abandon their* Imperial Chief. They know not the meaning of German loyalty nor how the German Federal Princes and races stand by the Emperor and the Empire with blood and iron to their last breath. They do not know that to us Germans military training is *no sacrifice but our greatest pride.*

We will have no starvation peace! In order to attain a speedy peace we must strengthen our nerves for endurance as Hindenburg bids. *If we willingly bear with distress and deprivation, the German people will gain a Hindenburg peace,* which will adequately repay the price of victory, terrible sacrifice, and exertion. Any other peace means a devastating blow to our future development. The stunting of our position in the world and accompanying intolerable burdens would destroy our commercial situation and all the prospects of our working classes. Instead of exporting valuable wares, Germany would then again see her sons emigrate in large numbers.

The Founders of the German Vaterlands-Partei have requested His Highness the Archduke John Albert of Mecklenburg and the Grand Admiral von Tirpitz to become the leaders of the party.

To all who subscribe to these views we appeal to join the German Vaterlands-Partei. Anyone wishing to help is welcome. The aims of the party must be realized at once. Not a moment is to be lost.

Germany's salvation, honor, and future is at stake!

KÖNIGSBERG IN PRUSSIA, on the Day of Sedan, 1917

THE REICHSTAG AND THE
TREATY OF BREST-LITOVSK,
MARCH 18, 1918

Throughout the war, Germany sought to bring Russia to terms by contradictory techniques. On the one hand, Germany hoped that conservative, pro-German elements at the Czar's court would win the upper hand and negotiate a separate peace. On the other hand, Germany encouraged revolution in Russia in the hope of bringing about the Russian Empire's collapse. It was the latter policy which succeeded, and it was the German General Staff which permitted Lenin to travel across Germany in the famous sealed railroad train which brought him to Russia and which paved the way for the Bolshevik Revolution of November 1917. Subsequently, the Germans and the new masters of Russia negotiated at Brest-Litovsk. The chief Russian negotiator, Trotsky, hoped to use the negotiations to expose the imperialism of the Germans and promote revolution in central and western Europe. The German negotiators tried to appropriate Wilsonian and Leninist slogans appealing to nationalism and the self-determination of peoples to separate the Baltic provinces and the Ukraine from the Russian Empire. Within the German government there was, as usual, a conflict between the civilian authorities, represented by Foreign Secretary Baron von Kühlmann, and the military, represented at the negotiating table by General Max Hoffmann. The former sought to moderate a few of the terms and above all the methods of German expansionism. When Trotsky protested against German demands by withdrawing from the negotiations in early February 1918 and declaring that Russia would neither make war nor peace, Ludendorff launched an offensive, compelled the Bolsheviks to resume negotiations, and forced Kühlmann to dictate terms to the Russians. Furthermore, after the treaty was signed in March 1918, the Germans remained dissatisfied, imposed further onerous economic and political terms in supplementary treaties and invaded the Crimea.

The Reichstag reaction to the Treaty of Brest-Litovsk has been viewed as a test of the sincerity of the peace resolution of July 1917. Count von Hertling, who had replaced Michaelis as Chancellor in November 1917, tried to defend the treaty as a realization of the principle of self-determination (Document 16) and the representative of the Foreign Office, Baron von dem Bussche, defended the way in which the Russians had been forced to terms (Document 17). The Center and Progressive parties, who had voted for the Peace Resolution, did not find it inconsistent to vote for the Treaty of Brest-Litovsk. The Social Democrats, as evidenced by Deputy Eduard David's speech (Document 18) were too disturbed by the terms of the treaty and the methods employed to refrain from criticism. Nevertheless, they decided to abstain rather than oppose the treaty since they were anxious for peace in the East, hoped that the treaty with the Ukraine would release valuable and much needed grain supplies, and did not want to ruin their parliamentary alliance in the Reichstag with the Center and Progressive parties. The National Liberals and Conservatives voted enthusiastically for the treaty. The National Liberal leader, Gustav Stresemann, presented a forthright defence of the treaty (Document 19), and his remarks are particularly interesting in the light of his subsequent career as Foreign Minister of the Weimar Republic (1924–1929) and recipient of the Nobel Peace Prize for his work in establishing friendly relations with France in the Locarno Treaty. Historians continue to debate who was the real Stresemann, the annexationist of the First World War or the Nobel Prize winner of the Weimar era. The Independent Socialist leader, Hugo Haase, was as blunt in attacking the treaty as Stresemann had been in defending it (Document 20), and only his party actually voted against the treaty. After the war, the Treaty of Brest-Litovsk and the Treaty of Versailles were often compared, and the former was frequently used to defend the latter. It was argued that in comparison to Brest-Litovsk, Versailles was mild and humane and that the Germans had earned the punitive measures of Versailles by their performance at Brest.

16   FROM   *Statement of Chancellor*
von Hertling in the Reichstag on the
Russian Peace

Gentlemen, when I spoke for the first time on this spot, on November 29 of last year, I was able to announce to the Reichstag that the Russian Government had sent a proposal to all the belligerent powers for entering into negotiations regarding an armistice and a general peace. We, together with our allies, accepted the proposal, and sent delegates to Brest-Litovsk as soon as possible. Those powers which up to that time were Russia's allies kept away.

The course of the negotiations is known to you, gentlemen. You remember the endless speeches, which were intended not so much for the delegates who were gathered there as for the widest publicity, and which pushed further and further off the proper aim of our endeavor, an understanding, and the repeated interruptions, the discontinuance and the resumption of the negotiations. A point had been reached where a clear alternative had to be formulated. On March 3 the conclusion of peace took place at Brest-Litovsk, and on March 16 it was ratified by the competent assembly in Moscow. [*Applause.*]

It is not my intention to dilate on the judgment passed on the peace with Russia by enemy powers. When hypocrisy has become second nature [*"Quite right!"*] and untruthfulness has grown to brutality [*lively assent*], when at the very moment that an oppressive hand is about to be laid on a neutral country, they dare to speak of pursuing an entirely unselfish policy, every attempt at calm discussion and every objective consideration is bound to fail. [*Lively applause.*] If a telegram from Washington thought fit to express to the Congress assembled at Moscow the sympathy of the United States at the moment, as it declares, "when the

SOURCE (16). Reprinted from *Fall of the German Empire, 1914–1918,* Volume I, pp. 774–777, edited by Ralph Haswell Lutz with the permission of the publishers, Stanford University Press. Copyright 1932 by the Board of Trustees of the Leland Stanford Junior University.

German power has thrust in to interrupt and frustrate the whole struggle for freedom" [*Haase: "Of course! Finland!" Cries from the Majority: "Quiet! Is he a German?"*], then I put that calmly aside with the rest. [*Chairman calls for order.*] We have not for a moment contemplated, and do not contemplate, opposing the justified wishes and endeavors of Russia liberated from Tsarism. As I said on November 29 we desire for that sorely tried land a speedy return of peaceful and orderly conditions, and we deeply deplore that this still seems remote and that terrible conditions have made their appearance in many places.

I now turn to the treaty itself. As you will immediately perceive, it contains no conditions whatever dishonoring to Russia, no mention of oppressive war indemnities, and no forcible appropriation of Russian territory. [*Shouts from the Independent Socialists.*] That a number of the border states have severed their connection with the Russian state is in accordance with their own will which was recognized by Russia. In regard to these states we adopt the view formerly expressed by me that under the mighty protection of the German Empire they can give themselves a political form (*Staatliche Gestaltung*) corresponding to their situation and the tendency of their *Kultur,* while, of course, at the same time safeguarding our interests.

In Courland this development has gone the farthest. As you know, a few days ago a deputation sent by the Courland Landesrat, the body which is recognized as competent, came and announced the severance of the country from its previously existing political connections, and expressed the desire for a close economic, military, and political connection with Germany. In the reply with which the Kaiser charged me as the lawful representative of the Empire, I recognized the autonomy of Courland and both thankfully and joyfully took cognizance of its desire to lean on the German Empire, which desire, in fact, corresponds to the old cultural relations, which go back for centuries; but I reserved a final decision on the political form until the conditions there have been further consolidated and until the constitutionally competent factors on all sides have decided upon their future attitude in this connection.

As regards Lithuania, a resolution providing for a close attachment (*Anschluss*) to the German Empire by an economic and military connection was arrived at last year. During the next few days I expect a deputation from the National Council there which will announce anew this decision, after which similar recognition of Lithuania as an independent (*unabhängig*) state organism will follow. We calmly await its further political development.

In Livonia and Esthonia, however, things are somewhat different. Both of these provinces lie east of the frontier line agreed upon in the peace treaty. They are, however, as Article 6 of the peace treaty with Russia says, to be occupied by a German policing force until security is guaranteed by their own institutions and until their public order is restored. The moment for a new political orientation will then have come for these countries also. We hope and desire that they, too, will then place themselves in close and friendly relationship with the German Empire, but in such a way that this will not exclude peaceable and friendly relations with Russia.

Now a few words about Poland, which, it is true, is not expressly mentioned in the peace treaty. As is already well known, it was the proclamation of the two Emperors of November 5, 1916, which announced to all the world this country's independence. It follows, therefore, that the further shaping of this new state can take place only on the basis of joint negotiations between Germany and Austria-Hungary on the one hand and Poland on the other. Suggestions for the shaping of our future relationship have recently reached the Government and the members of the Reichstag from political circles in Poland. We shall now gladly examine whether, and to what extent, these proposals are reconcilable with the aims pursued by the two Governments, which are directed toward living permanently in good and neighborly relations with the newly-arisen state whilst at the same time safeguarding our own interests. Further information will be given by Herr von dem Bussche.

I conclude. When, as I do not doubt, you sanction the treaties now laid before you, and when shortly peace with Rumania is also concluded, then what I ventured to predict on February 24 as an impending event will have become an established fact. Then peace will have been restored on the entire Eastern front [*"Bravo!"*]; but let us indulge in no delusions. World peace is not yet an accomplished fact. In the Entente States not the slightest inclination to terminate the terrible business of war is yet perceptible. Their aim seems still to be to fight on until we are destroyed. We shall not, however, lose courage. [*Loud cheers.*] We are prepared for every contingency, and we are ready to make further heavy sacrifices. [*Renewed loud cheers.*] God, who has been with us until now, will continue to grant us His help. We have confidence in our just cause, in our incomparable army, and also in its heroic leaders and troops. We have confidence also in our steadfast nation. The responsibility, however, for further bloodshed will fall, as I said on February 24, on the heads of all those who desire the continuance of that bloodshed. [*Lively applause from Right, Center, and Left. Shouts from Independent Socialists. Renewed "Bravos!"*]

17   *von dem Bussche's*
              Statement in the Reichstag on the
              Russian Peace

Gentlemen, the allied Governments had recently the honor to submit to you the first peace treaty in this heaviest of all wars, namely the Ukraine Peace Treaty. These Governments submit to you now two further peace treaties with the Russian and the Finnish Governments. These treaties, as the Chancellor already remarked, make an end to the state of war on the Russian front, and when, as we may safely assume, peace will be concluded in the next few days with Rumania, then we shall soon have returned to peace, in principle, on the entire Eastern front. We owe this relief in the military and economic war situation primarily to the incomparable heroism of our troops and to the troops of our allies, as also to the brilliant leadership of our great generals. [*"Bravo!" and "Quite right!"*]

The reason why, after the conclusion of the second phase of the Trotsky period, we adopted a sharper tone and acted with

SOURCE (17). Reprinted from *Fall of the German Empire, 1914–1918,* Volume I, pp. 777–779, edited by Ralph Haswell Lutz with the permission of the publishers, Stanford University Press. Copyright 1932 by the Board of Trustees of the Leland Stanford Junior University.

more firmness in order to attain the desired result of peace cannot have been unknown to you. It soon became evident that Trotsky did not desire the conclusion of peace. He primarily desired to instigate our country to rebellion and he firmly counted on a revolution in Germany and Austria-Hungary to help him to veil the fact of the Russian defeat. He gave clear expression to his disappointment in this connection.

Trotsky never really negotiated at all. That he had no intention of bringing things to a conclusion we did not simply infer from his speeches and his behavior; we had other quite certain information to that effect. No choice was, therefore, left to us but to draw military conclusions from the breaking off of the negotiations by Trotsky and, when the desired effect immediately followed, to put our demands into a form which left no room for further protraction of the negotiations. It cannot therefore be wondered at that, in consequence of such an equivocal attitude on the part of our opponents, our demands should more than ever before aim at securing safeguards for our future and be raised in consequence.

The negotiators, who, this time without M. Trotsky, again arrived at Brest-Litovsk, realized the justice of our action in raising our demands. Our negotiators gained the impression that the Russians expected far more severe demands after they had, by their conduct, forced us to a fresh appeal to arms and to further considerable expenditure. If during the negotiations between March 1 and March 3 the Russians protested against our action and also made a further protest at their conclusion, declaring that they had been forced to accept our demands without sufficient time for the negotiations, that was assuredly done more to save their own faces than from any real conviction. Without doubt they pursued the tactics decided upon in Petrograd before their arrival in order to brand us with the annexationist and militarist stamp and to represent themselves as the champions of peaceful ideas. I must again expressly state that their protest was entirely unfounded. In substance it was a question of our old demands which had been thoroughly discussed since December during long weeks of negotiations. All that was new, after our ultimatum, was the demand regarding Kars, Ardahan, and Batum.

In the plenary session of March 1, Herr von Rosenberg not only submitted to the Russian Delegation a draft of the political agreement and discussed it article upon article but also gave them a Russian translation. Excellency v. Korner, too, explained on the same day the draft for an agreement upon economic relations, and made it clear to them that the demands were held entirely within the scope of the previous negotiations and the ultimatum. He, too, submitted a Russian translation. This was also done by Excellency v. Kriege with regard to the legal question. In submitting to the Russian Delegation the Russian text of the German-Russian supplementary treaty, he stated to them that this draft is based in all essential points upon the results of the previous negotiations of the Russian-German Legal Commission. All this shows that the Russian Delegation was well acquainted with the material of the Treaty. Thus in the discussion on March 2 and 3 they repeatedly pointed out inexactitudes in the translations supplied by us and otherwise also showed a thorough knowledge of the Peace Treaty. [*"Hear, hear!"—Right.*] The Russian Delegation's assertion that it had no time for adequate study of the peace terms is, therefore, quite untenable. The Russians had no intention of thoroughly examining the draft treaty, because at the sitting of March 1 the Russian First Delegate, Sokolnikov, without giving any reason, rejected the proposal to form special commissions for legal and economic matters. Besides, the Russians had brought no experts with them, as Sokolnikov himself admitted. As regards details, of both the main political treaty and the economic and legal supplementary treaties, I may refer you to the memorandum which is now in your hands, and I may add that in all essentials it agrees with the provisions of the Ukraine Treaty, except for a few points which have been changed in our favor.

We had to conclude a separate peace treaty with Finland afterwards, in consequence of the recognition by the Russian People's Republic that Finland had left the existing Russian State and that Russia was therefore unable to conclude a peace with us on behalf of Finland. There is no doubt that Finland was entirely averse to the war forced upon us by Russia and our other opponents, but as part of the Russian State it found itself actually in a state of war with us. The negotiations with Finland took place in Berlin, and were marked by a spirit of conciliation. In this case, too, our interests had been preserved in a thoroughly advantageous manner by our negotiators, and a series of improvements was introduced as compared with the former state of affairs. [*"Bravo!"*]

18   *Eduard David's Speech*

We agree to the motions to refer both the treaties to the Committee. Otherwise our feelings toward the *Russian treaty* are very mixed. [*"Quite right!"—S.D.*] We, too, rejoice that all along the Eastern front fighting has come to an end. . . . . Still, we regret that the *peace of Brest-Litovsk* is not the result of a process of mutual agreement, but is obviously imposed *by force*. [*"Very true!"—S.D.*] At Brest-Litovsk not only the Bolsheviks but also our own diplomatists have given in to the representatives of armed force. [*"Very true!"—S.D.*] It is not because the Empire of the Tsars has gone to pieces that we are so critical of this treaty. When the Revolution broke out we did not imagine it to be our mission to preserve the unity of the Russian Empire, built up in centuries by an aggressive policy of the worst kind. [*"Very true!"—S.D.*] . . . . It was enough to remove the oppressive weight of the Tsar's Government for the national movement to come to the surface. This was one opportunity for a change in those districts inhabited by other races, for the people that so desired could make itself free; . . . . another was the intention of the Bolsheviks to permit self-determination to other races—even to the extent of separation from the Empire. Our diplomatists should have achieved this by an agreement; but they failed because they did not understand the Bolshevik motives. . . . . The need for peace was strongly felt throughout Russia.

The Bolsheviks could put up with the loss of the stranger populations of the marches, but not at the hand of Prussian military power, nor in a way that violated democratic principles. . . . . This road was barred by the declaration of the German

SOURCE (18). Reprinted from *Fall of the German Empire, 1914–1918,* Volume I, pp. 779–783, edited by Ralph Haswell Lutz with the permission of the publishers, Stanford University Press. Copyright 1932 by the Board of Trustees of the Leland Stanford Junior University.

Delegation on December 27 that self-determination of the marches in the sense of separation from Russia must be accepted as an accomplished fact. The victor's sword, thrown into the scale by General Hoffmann, increased the difficulty.

When Germany has once accepted *"self-determination"* she must also risk its dangers. . . . . But we were not strong enough for that. That is why this treaty has not evoked the expected enthusiasm but, on the contrary, a great uneasiness. . . . . [*"Very true!"*—*S.D.*] Faith in German political honor is shaken; the name Brest-Litovsk is being used to smother any desire for peace in France and England. . . . . Enemies of the Bolsheviks taunt them with treason toward Russia, and the party of the Bolsheviks has divided. . . . . No future Russian Government will accept this peace with sincerity. Lenin has stated that this peace is not final, was forced upon them, and is only provisional. . . . . There is no security that this peace will last. The war is finished, but not the hostility. The Entente is already engaged in repairing the Eastern break in the ring. We have made our chief task—the break-up of the hostile coalition—not easier, but harder.

. . . . We have even helped the formation of a new coalition. *England's object in the war*—to unite her African colonial empire with India—is made easier by this treaty. . . . . Mitteleuropa is an inland state and, as regards world economics, a small inland state in comparison with the world-wide empires of England, America, and East Asia. . . . . We can rob the Brest-Litovsk treaty of some of its dangers if we follow it up by giving the right of self-determination to the marches [*"Quite right!"*—*S.D.*] and allow as many of the inhabitants as possible to share in the settlement of their domestic constitution. Thus we should snatch a very forcible argument away from a hostile Great-Russian Government. Afterwards Russia could, in that case, accommodate itself to circumstances, without prejudice to its honor. . . . . The arrangement of the affairs of the marches is, then, the touchstone of German honor. In November the Chancellor himself said, "You cannot push nations to and fro against their will, as if they were pieces in a game." . . . .

Unfortunately it looks as if our actions in the East were not in agreement with these repeated declarations of the Chancellor. [*"Very true!"*—*S.D.*] We must have security that the actions of the Government fit its words; as yet, that does not seem to be the case. ["*Very true!*"—*S.D.*] There is a hostile party in Germany whose aims are opposed to those of the Government. ["*Quite right!*"—*S.D.*] It commands an influential press, the Pan-German, Conservative, Annexationist papers. It desires expansion in the East, not as security for our frontiers but as annexations. It will not hear a word about a popular franchise in the marches. It fears that such a franchise might affect Prussia. . . . . Among its agents are also many officials of the military government in the Baltic lands. . . . . This divergence of views must not be forgotten. We are convinced the civil government is sincere in what it says; but has it the power to carry out its plans? . . . . Through Poland, Lithuania, and Courland the policy of the military is at cross-purposes with that of the Government. The whole wretched tale of our Polish policy from the date of the Kaiser's proclamation is explained by this divergence of opinion. Now it seems that the difficulty about Cholm has been smoothed over in Vienna. But the military party aim at a great annexation on the Polish west frontier on the plea of securing our boundary. But military security that produces enduring enmity in a neighbor is a mockery of military security. ["*Very true!*"—*S.D.*] . . . .

In Lithuania, also, the exertions of the military party have aroused great distrust and counter movements which we regret. . . . . The Lithuanians desired that a Diet should be convened by a general, equal, and direct vote. To achieve their own ends the military party actually stopped communications between the Chancellor and the Lithuanians. A letter from the President of the Lithuanian Landesrat that had to pass the military government of the Baltic lands has up to today not reached the Chancellor. ["*Hear, hear!*"—*S.D.*] Thus the Chancellor's letters are held up by the superior military commandant who does not approve his policy. . . . . They wish to make Lithuania an east-Elbe colony, which is to renounce popular government. Because the Lithuanians refused, the military party has, so far, prevented the recognition of their independence. . . . . That contradicts the promises made to the border peoples at Brest-Litovsk. ["*Quite true!*"] Can anyone believe that Lithuania can exist as an "east-Elbe" military colony beside the republic of the Ukraine? The Lithuanians are threatened with the division of their country. Who knows whether the military party will hold up the Lithuanian deputation that the Chancellor expects, as they did the above letter! There was formerly a permanent representative of the Lithuanian Landesrat in Berlin, but later the army withdrew his passport. . . . .

I deny that the Courland Landesrat is competent to speak in the name of the inhabitants. It relies on privileges granted by the Tsars. . . . . Now it has no legal standing, for in times of revolution the will of the people is the law. [*"Quite right!"—S.D.*] We recognized that in the case of the Ukraine and Russia. . . . . The decree of the Courland Landtag is no more than a deal made by the Prussian Junkers and the Baltic nobles and agreed to by part of the German-Lettish middle classes. . . . . We welcome the Chancellor's statement that this decision is not final, in opposition to the military party, who regard the decree as final and not to be revoked by a more democratic Landtag. . . . . Even under Russian rule Letts and Esthonians fought for independence. . . . . If their hopes are once again disappointed, they will cherish bitter hatred against their new lords and will find support in Great Russia's hostility to us. You must avoid such a policy if you really desire the safety and progress of the German elements in the Baltic lands. Artisans, small manufacturers, and peasants are not represented at all in the Lettish Landtag. . . . . Formerly the Baltic nobles were hand and glove with the worst reactionaries in Russia. The Russian armies that devastated East Prussia were led by Baltic nobles like Rennenkamp. . . . .

Significant was the remark of the Chancellor: "Our relations with Esthonia and Livonia must be so arranged as not to preclude friendship with Russia." That is the ground from which we take off. . . . . Further, the Chancellor refused to interfere in Finland's internal affairs. Here, too, is a glaring contradiction between the words of the civil government and the acts of the military. [*"Quite right!"—S.D.*] . . . . When the press says we must hurry to help the Finns against the Russians it is trying to lead the public astray. It is to be regretted that the Censor forbids the publication of the truth. The Red Guards in Finland are not Russians but Finns. [*"Hear, hear!"—S.D.*] These Finnish Red Guards are the force at the disposal of the Red Government. . . . . It is civil war in Finland, in which both parties claim to be the lawful authority. We hear stories of Red Guard atrocities in Finland, and it is true that the Red Government is doing its best to destroy some robber bands. There are daily in Berlin 300 cases of theft and assault ["*Hear, hear!*"—*S.D.*]; in the whole country there must be many thousands. What should we say if a foreign Power for this cause arrogated the right to invade us? . . . . ["*Very true!*"—*S.D.*] The same forces support the Red Government in Finland as support the Ukraine Government which we call our friend. What fierce hatred will be begotten in the working classes if their movement is crushed by German troops! According to the Norwegian press, Germany's object is to establish a monarchy under a German prince. This is denied. But the denial meets little credence; and our purposes with regard to Courland only strengthen the rumor. All along the Eastern front German policy has destroyed the sympathy of the masses for Germany. . . . . This policy is a declaration of war against all popular forces, against those sections of the marches that desire independence. Should the shortsighted brute force of the military party carry the day against the declarations of the Chancellor, the inevitable result would be that the whole district from the Baltic would become a smoldering furnace where all would resist German influence. We refuse to be brought up against such a situation.

. . . . It is now clear that the Pan-Slav movement had no root in the people. This policy of brute force would beget a new Pan-Slav movement—with support in Austria—the object of which would be the destruction of the German policy of domination known abroad as Pan-Germanism and at home as Pan-German force policy. By so doing we should authorize the Entente to put themselves at the head of the opposition to such a policy of force. Therefore, the Reichstag and the Government must make head against an irresponsible party which, apparently, is determined to become supreme in the Empire. . . . . Brute force does not win hearts.

Only a freedom-loving policy can bring order in the East; only an agreement on popular lines can lay the foundation of order in the East. In this way a stronger peace will be secured; a peace resting on the power of the sword is the weakest peace known. Germany cannot solve the problems presented in its general policy by the methods and ways of the old Prussian ruling caste. Peace at home, peace abroad can be won only through right and freedom. [*Applause from the S.D.*]

19   *Gustav Stresemann's Speech*

Gentlemen, yesterday Dr. David criticized the treaty with Russia very sharply as one won by superior force. . . . . The German people, he said, is very uneasy over it and fears that Russia's weakness will only help England by giving free play to its expansion in Asia. . . . .

At once Dr. Naumann showed that this was not so, that Russia's decay was already complete. Dr. David contradicts his own party, which admits that Russia was ruined not by the German arms but because it was impotent even before the war. . . . . What elements are there in Russia today with whom we can make an alliance? Lenin, Trotsky and Company are working for a union of nations on the basis of a mutual understanding of the working classes throughout the world. . . . . Is it a restored Tsar? It is possible that the monarchical idea will come to the top again, ... but for the last twenty-five years and more the grand dukes have been the chief fomenters of hatred toward Germany. [*"Quite right!"*—*S.D.*] . . . . The Cadets or Octobrists? But when the Russian commercial treaties were being renewed this very section of the Russian middle classes fanned passion against Germany and demanded the closing of Russia against us. . . . . We have never exploited the difficulties of other nations for our own political ends. [*"Quite right!"*—*N.L.*] What thanks had we for our restraint toward Russia during her war with Japan? An alliance with our enemies; the assault of 1914. . . . The cause of Anglo-German friendship was pushed with warm-hearted eloquence. . . . . Italy absorbed Tripoli and France Morocco, yet we put forward no claims. . . . . Then followed the agreements between England and Russia—the division of Persia and China into spheres of interest—while we, who most covet expansion, yet stopped always in the shade, stood aside. Yet the consequence was the World War. Peace is not to be had by resigning all idea of expansion. We have respected the rights of neutrals, but we

SOURCE (19). Reprinted from *Fall of the German Empire, 1914–1918*, Volume I, pp. 783–787, edited by Ralph Haswell Lutz with the permission of the publishers, Stanford University Press. Copyright 1932 by the Board of Trustees of the Leland Stanford Junior University.

have won no friends. . . . . We laid the foundation of Italian unity, but Italy has surrendered Savoy and Nice to France and fights against us. [*"Quite right!"—N.L.*] . . . . Austrian neutrality in 1870 was not the result of the peace of Nikolsburg, but of our speedy victory in the early days of the war. [*Lively applause from Right and N.L.*] . . . . The re-establishment of the Empire with a population of 170 millions is in the cards, but as yet it is only a hope that may prove fallacious. Therefore a great responsibility rests on those who would favor the Tsar as the partner on whom we should rely in the East. . . . .

Another argument against the treaty is the future economic war. . . . . That must come, and United States capital will be used in it. It will hasten the coming of Chamberlain's Greater England; and France will take an enthusiastic part. . . . . I do not believe in an organized boycott of German goods; witness the preliminary treaties. . . . . The United States will not reject our trade, especially our potash. . . . . For its own sake Italy can take no part in such a war, and other states are too small. We must not be influenced by England's policy, which, now that her hope of victory is gone, is putting forward the economic war to frighten us into concessions in her favor. There is no need for fear. In the midst of war our exports might have been valued by thousands of millions had we so desired. We received offers of this kind from Americans and others. During our negotiations in the East we see how every nation desires German goods first.

I cannot approve Dr. David's criticism of the Brest-Litovsk treaty; we were on the horns of a dilemma. . . . . And I do not blame General Hoffmann for reminding the Russians that we were the victors. . . . . Herr Groeber has on this occasion raised no objections to General Hoffmann's signing the treaty; he was, in fact, the plenipotentiary. . . . . His remarks about Courland provoked me seriously. He spoke of an agreement between Prussian and Baltic Junkers. You cannot dismiss a great historical event by a catchword. [*"Quite right!"—Right and N.L.*] Deputies of the Social-Democrats have lately been bargaining with Baron Ronikier and Prince Radziwill, not as peers but as representatives of the Poles; in this case they took no exception to the fact that a Prince and a Count represented Poland. [*"Quite right!"— Right and N.L.*] . . . . We are not dealing with the Baltic barons alone, for the middle class is German in sentiment. . . . . Had the Baltic Germans wished to be absorbed in Russia, this would have happened long ago, as it has so often happened in America. . . . . It is not correct that this treaty has settled the affairs of Courland while another arrangement is in store for Esthonia and Livonia. . . . . Riga, the capital of Livonia, and the Esthonian islands lie inside the sphere of German interests. After the various deliverances of the Baltic peoples, a vote taken on a more popular basis is not—in my opinion—necessary. . . . . These peoples, through no fault of their own, as a whole are not ready for parliamentary institutions. . . . . So existing institutions—with the assistance of Letts and Esthonians—must be allowed to represent the country. . . . .

I view with apprehension the proposal to separate Courland, with Riga, from the rest of Livonia and Esthonia. . . . . Here the right of self-determination does not apply, for the Letts are the fiercest opponents of such a division. If it is intended that Riga and Courland should go with Germany while Livonia and Esthonia go with Russia, then, among other losses to Germany and the Baltic provinces, would be the loss by Riga of much of its importance; . . . . for Russian trade would be deflected to Reval. Livonians and Esthonians, as well as Germans, hold that the Baltic lands are one. May the Government not forget this! . . . .

We agree that Lithuania is to have its own government as soon as it is ready for it. . . . . The difficulty is that the influential people are the Polish landlords, and, in the towns, Poles and Jews, while educated Lithuanians are in the minority and in many cases live abroad. . . . . By an independent Lithuania we mean, of course, close connection with Germany under a military convention, customs union, and one system of money and communications, as the deputies desired. Full autonomy of such little nations belongs to Utopia. Normal development drives them into union with a bigger neighbor. . . . . I do not believe in Wilson's universal league of nations; I believe that, after the conclusion of peace, it will burst like a soap bubble. . . . . I have no objection to make to Lithuania's wish for a Catholic prince; in a Catholic land, Catholic officials also are desirable. One result of the war will be a better feeling between the two Churches in our own country. [*Applause by Center and N.L.*] . . . . There seems to me little hope of a good understanding with the Poles.

They do not see that they are the aggressors, not we. [*"Quite true!"*] . . . . It cannot be treated as a question of Poland only recognizing the *status quo* as regards Germany if Germany recognizes the *status quo* of Poland. I must protest against the suggestion—due to enemy politicians—that an international conference may be held to discuss Poland and Alsace-Lorraine. . . . . We cannot discuss whether Posen and West Prussia should belong to Germany. . . . . We do not wish to annex parts of Poland; but if our High Command tells us that we must improve our frontier by removing it farther east to prevent future invasions, no one will take on himself the responsibility of opposing such a need. [*Applause from the N.L.*]

In Finland our military action has not been an intrusion into party politics. Scandinavian Social-Democrats have proved that crowds of Bolsheviks were sent to massacre and pillage, just as in the Ukraine. . . . . If Sweden had sent help there would have been no need for Germany to come to the rescue. . . . . The economic importance of Finland is often underestimated; before the war we exported more goods to Finland than to Turkey. . . . . Unfortunately in the Russian treaty not sufficient attention was paid to our foreign interests. When the Russian Government has confiscated all bank deposits, even those of foreigners, we cannot fulfill its demands in Germany till we have sufficient security for our own demands. . . . . To waive all claim to an indemnity from Russia is not, in my opinion, to wear a halo of reconciliation. Rather it is a poor outlook for the German taxpayers if they alone must bear the crushing weight of this war. [*Lively applause.*] . . . . We owe the Eastern peace to our weapons alone. The solemn exhortation of the Chancellor to the Western Powers was summarily rejected. . . . . By the fault of our enemies two million Germans are dead and 150 billions of debt is piled up; where is the moral obligation to abide by the Reichstag's offer which they spurned? No! Our enemies must bear the full burden of the prolonged war: only in this way is there any prospect of shortening it. [*Applause of Conservatives and N.L.*] When the Chancellor said that our enemies must bear the responsibility of battles to come, I take it to mean they are responsible also for any change in our policy as to territorial questions and indemnities. . . . . The Dwina-Dnieper canal deserves the closest attention. It will shorten the journey from Odessa to Hamburg by

3,559 kilometers. . . . . The Eastern peace is a great asset in our war balance. Had not the Entente politicians frivolously played with the destiny of their countries, they would have accepted the chance of peace held out to them by the Chancellor. Let them be warned by Russia. [*Lively applause by N.L.*]

20   *Hugo Haase's Speech*

. . . . We have nothing to take back from what we said at the first reading, and in the committee, with regard to the peace treaty. Herr David said that his friends regarded it with mixed feelings; my "Fraktion" has only one feeling, that of shame [*disturbance, and stormy interruptions on the Right*] that a peace of the sword should have been ruthlessly forced on our eastern neighbor. [*"Quite right!"—Independent Socialists.*] . . . . Things in the East have been arranged in accordance with the mad wishes of the annexationist politicians. Herr Erzberger is of the opinion that the peace treaty is in accordance with the Reichstag resolution. . . . . Herr Groeber tried to represent the same thing today by chicanery. [*Vice-President Dr. Paasche: "You should not accuse a colleague of chicanery."*] What do Messrs. Scheidemann, Ebert, and David say to this interpretation of the resolution by their comrades of the "Fraktion"? . . . . But the gentlemen plant hope on the grave of hope. [*Lively shouts from all sides.*] One often heard formerly that Social Democracy was done for; but then it took an unexpected flight. Give us freedom of the press and freedom of assembly, and then you will see. [*Continuous cheering on the Left. Vice-President Dr. Paasche: "I beg you not to interrupt your own speakers." Laughter and "Quite right!"*]

The military party has once more gained an absolute victory, and it will also know how to profit by its victory in the future. [*"Quite right!"—Independent Socialists.*] The military had the

SOURCE (20). Reprinted from *Fall of the German Empire, 1914–1918,* Volume I, pp. 787–789, edited by Ralph Haswell Lutz with the permission of the publishers, Stanford University Press. Copyright 1932 by the Board of Trustees of the Leland Stanford Junior University.

upper hand in the negotiations, and they differed very widely from the principles of a democratic peace. . . . . This peace treaty has been very unfavorably received by the neutral press. . . . . This peace is only an armistice, during which great armaments will be collected, and will be followed by a fresh violent war. The Russian peoples are not liberated; they are only under fresh thralldom. . . . . One who knows Lithuania told me that everywhere in the country the peasants and workmen say, "If we were still under the Tsar now, we should kiss his policemen's feet." At the moment when the Courland barons trembled for their landed property they discovered their love for Germany [*laughter and shouts from the Right; "Quite right!"—Independent Socialists*] and sought friendship with those of their own class here. [*Repeated denials from Right.*] Estonia and Livonia cannot be detached from Russian sovereignty without an understanding with Russia. . . . . Behind the scenes the idea is to separate these countries from Russia and attach them to Germany. The National-Liberal resolution does not show even a spark of democratic spirit. A few more persons were added to the representative body, and that is the "broad basis." The resolution is conceived in the same spirit as that of the peace treaty. . . . . The trade unions and trade associations are oppressed in Poland as never before; that is the "freedom" which has been brought to Poland. . . . . By violating the peace treaty Armenian territory is being attached to Turkey; . . . . if they had the free right of self-determination, the Armenians would resolve anything rather than association with Turkey. We are all sufficiently aware of how the Turks rage against the Armenians and stop at nothing in order to exterminate them. . . . . The peace treaty with Finland is a pure pretext, for we are not at war with Finland. [*"Very true!"—Independent Socialists.*] . . . . Our proposal to withdraw the German troops from Finland, where they are helping to put down the National Government and its troops, was rejected by the Main Committee. This peace treaty could only have been intended to give a handle for our inroad into Finland. . . . . All those who sanction further war credits are responsible for this unprecedented misuse of them. . . . . Scheidemann's followers announced today that they will refrain from voting on the Russian treaty, but they represent us outside this House as traitors because we voted against the Ukrainian peace treaty.

[*"Very true!"—Independent Socialists.*] . . . . *Steps are being
taken everywhere against supposed remarkable Bolshevist "ma-
rauding bands," while at the same time such important treaties
are concluded with Bolshevist Governments. The movements of
German troops are not directed against marauders but against
the Russian Revolution. Who sows the wind must reap the
whirlwind.*

21   *Result of the Discussions at
Spa on July 2–3, 1918*

*Ludendorff took advantage of his victory in the East to launch
a series of major offensives in the West in the spring of 1918 designed to break through the Allied lines. These offensives were
successful tactically but they did not bring the desired strategic
breakthrough. In early July, Ludendorff was preparing for his
last and most unsuccessful offensive. Although it is difficult to
see how he could still have hoped for the kind of total victory
that would have made the realization of his war aims possible,
his persistence is amply demonstrated by the decisions made at
these discussions between the military and civilian authorities.*

THE POLISH QUESTION

The Austro-Polish solution is dead. Definite demands shall
immediately be made on Vienna:

(a) Austria-Hungary renounces a personal union (i.e., of the
Habsburg and Polish thrones).

(b) The Poles shall suggest a candidate.

(c) Germany will retain economic predominance in Poland.
Poland remains our territorial passage to the East.

SOURCE (21). Translated by the editor from *Ursachen*, 2. Unterausschuss,
Beilagen, Teil II, pp. 223–224.

(d) Germany retains dominant influence over the railroads.

(e) Poland will participate in the costs of the war.

(f) Germany demands of Poland the . . . territorial border strip. . . .

THE BELGIAN QUESTION

Belgium must remain under German influence so that it never again can come under Franco-English influence and serve as a military staging area for our enemies.

To this end the separation of Flanders and Wallonia, to be tied only by personal union and economic agreements, shall be demanded. Belgium shall be brought into the closest relationship with Germany through a customs union, a common railroad organization, and the like. Temporarily, a Belgian army shall not exist.

Germany will guarantee herself a long occupation with gradual withdrawal in such a way that the Flemish coast and Liège will be evacuated last. Complete evacuation will be made dependent upon Belgium's establishing the closest possible connection with us. . . .

PART ONE

Pre-1945 Documents and Interpretations
B. The Interpretations

22 FROM *Erich Otto Volkmann*

The first major examinations of German war aims arose in connection with the post-1918 Reichstag investigations of the causes of the German collapse in 1918. The Reichstag committee charged with the investigation commissioned experts to provide expert testimony. They were given access to some of the confidential files on the war aims question, and their conclusions were based on the kind of documentary evidence presented in the previous section.

The most significant documentary material and discussion was presented to the committee by Erich Otto Volkmann, a former army officer and annexationist, who was nevertheless willing to defend the German aims and present basic information in as objective a manner as possible given his point of view. He placed particular stress on the differences between Bethmann and the Supreme Command and, in a manner that was to be echoed after the publication of Fritz Fischer's book thirty-five years later, he complained about the one-sided emphasis on German war aims.

BETHMANN HOLLWEG AND THE SUPREME COMMAND

. . . after the turn of the year 1916/17 the Supreme Command assumed leadership of the struggle for a peace which would bring

SOURCE (22). Translated by the editor from E.O. Volkmann, "Die Annexions-fragen des Weltkrieges," *Ursachen*, 2. Unterausschuss, pp. 92–95 and 158–169.

Germany a great increase of power. Bethmann Hollweg and Czernin, who continued to hope for a peace of understanding despite the refusal of the German peace offer, soon found themselves hard pressed. Just as soon as the responses of the leading statesmen of the Entente to the German peace offer became known, Hindenburg, on December 23, 1916, sent a letter to the Chancellor concerning war aims *"on the basis of the present military situation."* He demanded Briey and Longwy with the adjoining Belgian ore fields, and also Liège. The rest of Belgium was to be brought into the closest possible dependence on Germany. The prospect of expansion in the East was also included.

The war aims of the Supreme Command were supplemented by the navy which sent the following demands on December 19, 1916: sovereignty over the Belgian coast and the coast of Courland including the islands of Ösel and Dagö.

On December 26 (Colonial Minister) Solf sent in his colonial program which was concerned primarily with the establishment of a German Central African Empire. It was supplemented by the proposals of the Chief of the Admiralty Staff for the acquisition of strategic bases.

On January 2, 1917 the Kaiser remarked . . . that he would also have to change his war aims as a consequence of the Entente's rejection of the peace note. France and Belgium could no longer count upon any concessions. The Flemish coast would have to become German.

Bethmann Hollweg no longer had the power to defend himself openly against the Supreme Command. Now he was compelled to resort to confidential negotiations with Czernin, with whom he shared a very similar view of the situation, concerning war aims.

On March 26 . . . there were secret negotiations between Bethmann Hollweg and Czernin concerning war aims. The result was a "resume" of March 27 signed by Bethmann and Czernin alone in which the restoration of the *status quo ante* was set down as the minimal program. In the case of a more favorable military situation, then German expansion in the East at Russian expense and Austro-Hungarian expansion primarily at Rumanian expense were to be considered.

In mid-April the Kaiser intervened in the war aims controversy. On April 17 he asked the Chancellor to do more to make sure that the idea of a peace without annexations did not go uncontradicted.

On April 18 the Chancellor presented guidelines for a peace with Russia which took a middle ground between the idea of a peace of renunciation represented by the left and the annexationist desires propagated by the right.

In response on April 20 the Kaiser demanded precisely defined war aims. The war aims question could no longer be handled in a dilatory manner. He, the Kaiser, would decide any differences of opinion between the Chancellor and the Supreme Command.

Hindenburg wrote to the Chancellor on the same day. He urgently insisted that the minimal and primary demands be established for the coming negotiations with Germany's allies and the eventual negotiations with the enemy.

On April 23 the well known Kreuznach discussions took place in the presence of the Kaiser.

To the protocol of the discussion Bethmann appended a handwritten statement to the effect that he had expressly pointed out at Kreuznach that the peace conditions set down there were unattainable if one did not succeed in dictating the peace. With regard to the war aims in Belgium, he emphasized that they could only be carried out if England were completely defeated, a point which was also conceded by the Supreme Command and the Admiralty Staff. . . .

Such was the state of affairs when the papal mediation effort began on June 26.

As is known, Bethmann used this opportunity to emphasize strongly Germany's readiness for peace to the Nuncio, Pacelli. On the question of German intentions toward Belgium, he presented the prospect of the restoration of complete independence under the condition that this independence would also be recognized by England and France. With regard to the question of territorial concessions to France in Alsace-Lorraine, Bethmann answered that the peace effort should not collapse over this question if France was truly desirous of peace. A way could be found in the form of mutual border rectifications.

This position of the Chancellor was taken without prior agreement with the Supreme Command. It was very conciliatory with regard to Belgium and above all Alsace-Lorraine. On the question of war aims in the East, the Chancellor expressed himself more cautiously. He argued that in view of the chaotic conditions in Russia and the absence of a government capable of negotiating, the chances of peace there seemed to be eliminated for the time being.

Bethmann was prevented from pursuing this path to peace any further by his downfall. The causes of this are known. It has been demonstrated that Bethmann's inclination toward a moderate peace (*Verzichtfrieden*) played a role. Primarily, it was this that proved decisive in determining the attitude of the Supreme Command and the right wing parties.

The sudden interruption of Bethmann's chancellorship was all the more tragic for him because just at that time there was a Reichstag majority for the peace of understanding toward which he himself was striving. The Peace Resolution provided the most favorable background imaginable for his and the Kaiser's declarations to Pacelli.

By means of Bethmann's fall, the optimistic supporters of extensive war aims and a victorious and annexationist peace, who were led by the Supreme Command, were triumphant. . . .

• • •

SUMMARY

The problem of annexationism must be evaluated in terms of its political effects abroad and at home. In both cases there arises the question as to its influence on the course of the war and its conclusion. The answer is made more difficult by the fact that it is not merely a question of establishing historical facts because a whole series of factors from the realm of competing world views come into play which are very difficult to evaluate.

From the standpoint of *foreign policy*, the unfortunate native German habit of viewing developments in the sphere of foreign relations from the standpoint of domestic politics has distorted the historical picture—unfortunately, by and large, in disfavor of our own people. The effort to one-sidedly shift the blame for the collapse to those with other political opinions has, in this case, brought Germany into suspicion, both at home and abroad, of having propagated annexationism and nationalist propaganda

more than our enemies. This view, which has spread abroad
frequently, has become a welcome weapon in the hands of our
enemies. The proof that it is false has been amply given, to be
sure . . . by the disclosures of the Soviet Union concerning the
annexationist goals of the Entente countries. Unfortunately, they
have received less attention at home and abroad than the passionate charges which have been raised on the German side
against the annexationist desires of Hindenburg and Ludendorff
and against the war aims of the Pan-Germans. One should be
ashamed of the fact that the accusations levelled against our own
leaders have of late received partial refutation from new publications abroad, above all in America.

Added to this is the fact that the German documents concerning
the World War have largely been made available for the deliber-
ations of the (Reichstag) Investigating Committee and also for
other studies. What was to be found which was damaging has
been published. Every annexationist proposal, however secret
or unimportant, has been registered in detail before the entire
world. Our enemies in the World War have not followed this
procedure. What we know of their annexationist aims is limited
to the indiscretion of the Soviet Government and the private
publications of American and English politicians. The archives
of the French and English governments remain closed. That does
not speak for a "good conscience." If they had something to say
which "unburdened" themselves and "burdened" the Germans,
they certainly would not have held it back.

Because of these considerations, an effort will be made in this
presentation to create the possibility of comparing the annexationism of our enemies and our own insofar as the few publications of the enemy side allow. This seems to be the least that
can be done in fairness to one's own people.

The first thing to establish in viewing the consequence of
annexationism in foreign affairs is that nationalist-annexationist
currents, which were led by the Pan-Germans, existed in Germany
even before the war, but they had not won the same influence
over the country which Pan-Slavism had in Russia and the Ir-
redenta had later in 1915 in Italy. The charge raised, not by our
own enemies but rather in our own camp, that the Pan-German
movement, as the most active champion of German striving for

power and expansionism, was one of the most significant causes
of the outbreak of the war, is not accurate, or at least greatly
exaggerated. The prewar German government did not take its
decisions according to the dictates of the Pan-German movement.
The assumption that the enemy was to a certain extent driven
into the war out of fear of the Pan-German movement is just as
false.

The falseness of this view is already demonstrated alone by
the fact that Russia and France entered the war with very definite
annexationist war aims, which had already been agreed upon
between them well before the beginning of the war. The Russian
government understood very well that the precondition for their
realization was a general European war.

The German and the Austro-Hungarian governments had no
positive war aims in an annexationist sense at the outbreak of
the war. If one had asked the Reich Chancellor and the State
Secretary for Foreign Affairs about their war aims in the first
days of the war, then they could not have answered anything
other than *"Self-preservation and defence of our severely threatened country against an overwhelmingly superior force."* And
the great mass of the people would also have known nothing else.

The French statesman would have mentioned Alsace-Lorraine;
the Russian, the Dardanelles; the English, the shattering of Germany's rising world power.

One can even raise the question as to whether the prewar Pan-
German movement was not partially defensive and is not to be
evaluated as a reaction against Pan-Slavism and the French idea
of *revanche*. But even if one does not pursue these ideas, one
must see it (i.e., Pan-Germanism) as a type of phenomenon deeply
rooted in the spiritual constitution of our age, which when compared with parallel phenomena in other lands in no way demonstrates more extreme tendencies.

It is hard to think of greater hypocrisy than when the Entente
becomes irate over the annexationism of the Central Powers.
The attempt has been made here to follow the development of
annexationism during the war on both sides, and it has been
found that the comparison, all things considered, comes out in
favor of the Central Powers. The annexationism of the Entente
. . . runs along a continuously direct line. In its chief goals—

Alsace-Lorraine, Germany's Polish provinces, the South Tyrol, the eastern Slavic provinces of Austria-Hungary, and until the Russian collapse, the Dardanelles—there was not the slightest deviation from the first day until the last day of the war. The governments, the political parties, and the peoples were largely in agreement concerning these plans. Only temporarily did other tendencies make themselves noticeable here and there, and these were then rapidly suppressed again. Actually, nowhere can one speak of a war aims debate such as existed in Germany.

At present there is no satisfactory evidence for the frequently repeated claim . . . that the Entente powers were inclined to renounce their annexationist plans and accept a peace on the basis of the *status quo ante* . . . in the course of 1917 and the beginning of 1918. Against it stands the fact that the responsible agencies in England, France and Italy never permitted even the slightest indication that they wanted to renounce Alsace-Lorraine and the South Tyrol. Indeed, they proclaimed their annexationist desire at that time in a form which left no doubt about their determination. . . .

Conditions among the Central Powers are just as confused . . . as they are simple and clear on the side of the enemy. At no time during the war was there a united stand on the war aims question. In fact, in the second half of the war there actually was a chaotic situation which was made worse by the differences of opinion among the responsible agencies and the lack of clarity and weaknesses of the political leadership. It is obvious that this situation had fateful consequences for the foreign policy of the Empire. The extent of these consequences is a question which cannot be determined from the perspective of the problem of annexations alone. This much is certain, that according to everything we know of the plans and intentions of the Entente, satisfactory declarations concerning Belgium alone would not have sufficed to bring about an understanding. Only if the Central Powers would have been willing to give up Alsace-Lorraine and the South Tyrol could a peace have been had. . . .

Nevertheless, the lack of clarity of the German position on Belgium remains most regrettable even for those who do not give it decisive importance. The desire to establish responsibility not in a moral but in a political sense seems justified. It belongs above all to the statesmen and the highest leadership which did not find the strength to set forth a clear line and to carry it through by placing their entire persons behind it. Statesmanship which made a supreme virtue of engulfing the Belgian question in a fog of completely unclear conceptions in such a way that the supporters of completely opposite views were put in the position of believing that the government supported their position . . . does indeed invite the strongest criticism. . . . That, as far as one can tell, the possibility of peace was not destroyed lay . . . only in the fact that in the last analysis not the question of Belgium but rather the question of Alsace-Lorraine was the insoluble problem. . . . But even if one can at least exonerate the German Government on this score, there still remains the very unhappy side effect that the Entente was given a most welcome opportunity to let their own annexationist plans stay in the background while they loudly proclaimed Germany as the guilty party. This tactic continues to be effective to the present day.

Insofar as the eastern war aims are concerned, here there appears after 1915 goals similar to those pursued by Russia at the beginning of the war, namely the reunification of all the parts of Poland. The only question was to whom this newly created Poland would belong and what form the "connection" would take. That the Central Powers . . . made solemn promises to Poland without themselves having the slightest idea of what actually was to become of the land constitutes a political procedure which makes all criticism superfluous. It took its revenge by making an understanding and a separate peace with Russia, which might have been had shortly before the revolution, uncommonly difficult, indeed almost impossible. . . .

The problematical character of the Peace of Brest-Litovsk should not be laid entirely at the door of the statesmanship of the Central Powers. Insofar as the Entente Powers turned down the invitation of the Central Powers and Soviet Russia to enter negotiations on the basis of a peace of understanding, they participated in a certain sense in the responsibility for what had to occur. . . . It was self-understood that under all circumstances a strong buffer had to be created against this bubbling revolutionary cauldron and that in a time when the military decision was being sought in the West there had to be security in the East.

It was a provisional situation in which the military point of view was decisive. Probably it would have been well if the provisional character had been more clearly emphasized at the beginning in order to spare the German people and the entire world the lamentable and laughable negotiations over the future form of state for Poland, Courland, Lithuania, etc.

The Supreme Command has often been viewed as the driving element in these unhappy events. Now that we are already at a distance from the immediate impressions of the war and see the consequences more clearly, there is not much difference of opinion over the fact that their urgent desire to expand the power and territory of Germany carried them too far. But whoever puts himself back in wartime with its enormous psychic influences, pictures the weakness, indeed emptiness, of Germany's political leadership, and takes into account the annexationist and destructive desires of the enemy, will find an explanation for much of what occurred. The final explanation probably lies in the character and world view of Ludendorff. . . .

Within these very hastily sketched general bounds can be found the consequences of German annexationism in the area of foreign affairs. In general one can say: no matter how much one may criticize German war aims policy, no matter how much one may level accusations against individual political and military personalities . . . they did not have decisive importance for the course and outcome of the war.

In contrast it is to be established that the annexationist desires of the Entente countries influenced the development and end of the war in a completely decisive manner from the very outset.

The consequences of the annexation question in the realm of domestic politics can be briefly summarized by saying that it deepened conflict and division in our people and, insofar as it did this, contributed in no small way to our collapse. This fact will have to be granted, but whoever wants to add the problem of who was responsible for this will have to employ the greatest caution. While it might be permissable for the politician and moralist to make moral comments on the existence of imperialist-annexationist and socialist-pacifist currents and the unavoidable conflict between them which constitutes the fate of our age, this historian must approach these phenomena from another point of view. In any case, however, justice requires that one does not

deal with the question of responsibility in a one-sided way. Whoever wants to fix the responsibility will have to accuse both sides.
There is no reason why the annexationist, the convinced supporter of power politics, should have less of a right to propagate
his views than the representative of pacifism, the supporter of
the idea of international justice. . . .

The charge that the Pan-German movement alone sowed hatred
and mistrust among the people . . . arises from too one-sided a
perception of the situation. The same accusation can be made
from the other side and has been made. Whether this was done
with greater or lesser justification can be left aside.

Also one cannot blame the annexationists one-sidedly for the
initiation of the war aims debate. It has been shown that the
large majority of the people were inclined toward annexationism
after the first great successes, a phenomenon which naturally
was not only a consequence of Pan-German propaganda but
rather which is chiefly to be explained as a natural consequence
of war psychosis. After a sobering has taken place, the conflict
over war aims began in the spring of 1915. It is hardly possible
to attribute the initiative to one side or the other. In the last
analysis it is a matter of parallel development.

No party has the right to reproach the other even in the form
of the conflicts. The opponents of annexationism employed methods of fighting which were just as bad as those employed by the
Pan-Germans and the Fatherland Party. One may certainly be-
moan the fact that the German people in its fateful hour did
not maintain greater self-discipline and dignity . . . but to burden
one's political opponent one-sidedly with responsibility for this
is a demonstration of little self-awareness.

The conflict between the annexationists and their opponents
never came to a decision. Even Ludendorff was unable to prevent
either the Peace Resolution or the Central Powers' offer of a
peace of understanding on the basis of the status quo on December 25, 1917.

In this continuing stalemate one finds the tragic moment
in the problem of annexationism. Because of it the strength of
the government was weakened and the moral fiber of the people
was damaged. Any other solution would have been better.

It is at this point that one can perhaps attribute culpability
if one wants to raise the question of culpability at all. One cannot

reproach those who stood up for their convictions and fought for them. But one can certainly raise the question of ultimate responsibility for the highest leadership of the Reich which was unable to overcome the destructive condition of uncertainty.

For the purpose of comparison one need only be reminded of with what unshakable determination the statesmen of the Entente, and to be sure almost without regard to political position, maintained their program of crushing the Central Powers and extensive annexations and with what energy they fought every other type of idea. They owe their final success to this strong, purposeful leadership.

Lloyd George and Clemenceau are classic examples of this approach. On the other side, one must grant to Count Czernin that as an honest man he maintained with great consistency the position calling for an understanding which he regarded as the right one. That he failed in his intentions was not his fault but rather the result of overwhelming circumstances.

In Germany things were much less clear. Bethmann Hollweg personally tended toward a peace of understanding, but his policy spread the seeds of the German policy of annexationism of the last years of the war. It has been shown here that even in the Belgian question, especially the Flemish policy, but also in the policy of border states the basic lines had already been laid down under his full responsibility when Hindenburg and Ludendorff took over leadership of the annexationist cause. Nothing promoted the conflict over annexationism more than Bethmann's continuous effort to mediate between the two points of view and his continuous concessions to both sides. In war one needs a firm guiding hand and a clear, broad policy, and this was all the more necessary for Germany because the supreme leader, the Kaiser, was not a strong natural leader.

The question as to whether Hindenburg and Ludendorff had a moral right from the viewpoint of domestic politics to fight for a peace of victory and conquest is not discussable for me. It is just as unrewarding to debate over whether or not they exceeded their "competence." Questions of competence in the last analysis are only valid for normal circumstances and average human beings. Exceptional circumstances and above average men of great determination create their own laws.

Both men have been reproached for employing an unbearable

and immoral pressure by threatening to resign in critical situations, also in the matter of war aims, and thereby forcing the Kaiser to give way. One cannot see what else they, as strong, honest men, could do other than present their resignations when things took a course for which they did not believe they could take responsibility. It would perhaps have been better if the statesmen had represented their convictions with the same strength and the same decisiveness. Should one derive an accusation against the stronger party from the failure of the weaker one?

But in any case even the strong will . . . of Ludendorff did not suffice to guide things completely along the lines he wished. To the very end there remained a situation of stalemate such as existed in none of the enemy countries. The nature of the Kaiser did not permit anything else.

This once again supports the contention that the problem of leadership was fateful for Germany also in the question of annexations. None of the men in positions of responsibility rose as far above the other as was demanded by the dangers to the Fatherland. . . .

23   FROM   *Arthur Rosenberg*
The Birth of the German Republic, 1871–1918

One of the members of the Reichstag committee was the then Communist deputy, Arthur Rosenberg, whose Birth of the German Republic, 1871–1918, *remains the most brilliant and basic analysis of the structural problems leading to the collapse of the German Empire in 1918. As might be expected, Rosenberg placed particular emphasis on the relationship between domestic politics and the conflict over war aims. Although critical of Bethmann Hollweg, he classifies him as a "moderate" compared to Ludendorff and places special emphasis on the unhappy consequences of the latter's dictatorship. Although questions have*

SOURCE (23). Reprinted from *The Birth of the German Republic 1871–1918* by Arthur Rosenberg, translated from the German by Ian F D Morrow and published by Oxford University Press, pp. 98–109.

been raised about the extent of Ludendorff's dictatorship in domestic affairs by recent scholarship and Rosenberg has been corrected in many details, his account remains the classic study of the German Empire's persistent crisis.

The true interests of Germany from 1914 to 1916 demanded that peace on the basis of the *status quo* should be concluded as speedily as possible with both France and Russia. The conflict with England was of a more complicated nature. The English middle class had seized the opportunity afforded them by the war to extirpate German competition abroad. It was with this object that the German colonies and German property abroad were confiscated, the overseas interests of German firms liquidated, and every commercial link between Germany and the outer world severed. The destruction of German commercial competition was the common object uniting England with the great Dominions of the British Crown. It is only necessary to recall the part played by the Australian Prime Minister, Hughes, in the inception of an economic war against Germany. But in order to attain her object England had first to smash the military and political power of Germany. Hence the destruction of German militarism, i.e. of the German army and navy, became England's chief object in the war—an object in comparison with which territorial changes in the map of Europe were of little importance in the eyes of English statesmen. The only way in which England could have been brought to abandon this aim would have been by its finding itself opposed by the entire united force of Europe. But a European alliance could only have been attained were Germany to make good amidst the thunder of the cannon the mistakes of the Imperial policy since 1890. An understanding with France and Russia would have been necessary in order to force England to open the overseas markets to the European nations. It was in the interest of the German working class no less than in that of the middle class that Germany should be given her share in world commerce. The great masses of the German people looked upon England as their principal enemy throughout the war.

The German Government should never have permitted the childish and tactless ebullition of feeling symbolized in *Gott strafe*

England. They should instead have aroused in the nation at large the conviction that a victory over England was only possible if Germany were to pursue a conciliatory policy towards France and Russia. The nation should from the outset have been given to understand that Germany, even after the conclusion of a separate peace with France and Russia, could never hope to bring the British Empire with its overwhelming sea-power to its knees, and that the utmost that was to be achieved was a compromise. If the Government, on the other hand, were of the opinion that Germany was too weak even to force England to accept a compromise, and that a reconciliation with England was at all costs necessary, then it should have conducted German foreign policy in a manner that was likely to result in the achievement of that end. It was the duty of the Government to have impressed the necessity of such a policy upon the German nation. William II and Bethmann-Hollweg followed neither of these courses and pursued no definite policy. The terrible stupidity and aimlessness that characterized German foreign policy from 1890 to 1914 survived the outbreak of the war. The declarations on the part of the German Government from time to time that it did not desire conquests, or that it wished to secure the future of Germany in the coming peace, were of little value for purposes of foreign policy. In confidential circles Bethmann-Hollweg often emphasized the necessity for a separate peace with France and Russia, yet his public declarations and conduct of foreign policy resulted in rendering peace with Russia impossible.

The weakness of the Imperial Government could perhaps have been overcome by proposals or protests on the part of the nation. But for any such action the most important condition was lacking: the nation was ignorant of the true state of affairs. Not that the military communiqués were to blame for their ignorance. Enough has already been said above as to the extraordinary communiqués issued by Moltke and Stein. Under their successors, Falkenhayn and Ludendorff, from the end of September 1914 until the Armistice the communiqués were thoroughly accurate and reliable. These communiqués contained all that a report of this nature can be expected to contain, namely, indications as to where the Front lay and as to the most important events that had taken place. It is obvious that the really decisive factors in a military situation can never be made known in communiqués: the relative strengths of the opposing armies and of their reserves, and the whole strategical situation as it evolves from day to day. Neither the nation nor the members of the Reichstag learnt anything of the true strategical position which was known only to the Court, to the Great General Staff, and always to the Imperial Chancellor. Outside that limited circle no one knew anything. The ignorance of the public as to the true state of affairs was increased by the circumstance that the German armies were everywhere fighting on enemy soil and were everywhere in occupation of important enemy territory. The objective in a war is the opposing army and not the enemy's territory. The victor is he who has overthrown his enemy. From a military standpoint it is a matter of little importance where the decisive battle takes place. The elder Moltke, for example, had prepared a plan for the eventuality of a Franco-German war by which the French were to be allowed to invade Germany and to be decisively beaten at Frankfurt-am-Main. It was only the chance result of military operations in 1914 and 1915 that brought the German army into Belgium and Poland, and if an alteration had taken place in the extremely critical situation, the German troops might have found themselves compelled to evacuate these countries. The Imperial Government nevertheless did absolutely nothing to educate the German nation as to the highly precarious nature of the so-called "conquests" made by the German troops. The bulk of the population was convinced that the occupied districts were at the disposal of Germany.

The deception thus practised on the nation arose from the patriarchal nature of the relationship between the Government and the people. The uttermost publicity as to the military situation obtained in England throughout the entire war. The nation and the Press were able to discuss openly and informedly both good and bad developments. It would have been as absurd for the governing English middle class to have secrets from itself as for a business man to be afraid to draw up a balance sheet. The German Government, on the contrary, held it to be necessary to keep up the spirit of its subjects by letting everything appear in the best light. They feared that any knowledge of unpleasant events might injure the authority of the State. The German Government behaved like an anxious father who hesitates to tell his wife and children when things are going badly in his business. Still more remarkable than the touching-up of the military situation is the fact that the German nation was not permitted to know anything whatever as to the state of its health throughout the war. Silence was maintained as to the many thousand deaths that occurred among the civilian population in consequence of the blockade. The nation was officially assured that rationing was good for its health. A popular government which understood mass-psychology would have placarded every street corner with lists of those who died from famine in order to increase the bitter feeling against the enemy. It is only necessary to recall how England made use of the Zeppelin attacks on English towns in order to stimulate the fighting spirit of the nation.

The ignorance of the German people as to the true state of affairs showed itself in the way in which various sections of the populace regarded the war and the coming peace. The German industrialists hoped that a German victory would enable them to obtain their raw materials with greater ease. The mine-owners followed the German advance through Belgium and northern France with anxious eyes in the hope that the coal- and iron-mines in Luxembourg, Belgium, and Longwy-Briey would come into German hands. The industrialists in general demanded from the Government the annexation of Longwy-Briey, and also that of Belgium or at the very least its economic domination by Germany. They thus pursued the same tactics in war as in peace. Prior to 1914 certain great firms had compelled the German Government to lend the support of the Empire to their foreign undertakings. Now they demanded of it that it should realize as many as possible of their desires in the coming peace. If a middle-class industrialist party had itself been responsible for the government of Germany, it would also have been responsible for giving effect to the desires of its own members and would therefore have had to ask itself which, if any, of those desires were capable of realization. As it was, the Imperial Constitution afforded the industrialists the opportunity of presenting their demands without any consequent responsibility for their fulfilment. It was the business of the Government to put them into practice.

While the industrialists wished to augment their business opportunities in the west the Prussian landowners had similar plans for the furtherance of their own interests in the east. They hoped to acquire the thinly-populated agrarian districts of Courland and Lithuania for the settlement of the younger sons of German farmers, and for this purpose they sought to get into touch with the nobility of German origin in the Russian Baltic provinces. They hoped by means of an extension of Germany towards the north-east to strengthen the power of the aristocratic landed Prussian governing class within Germany itself. It is true that a number of the Prussian Conservatives preferred a separate peace with Imperial Russia to such projects.

It was of special importance in view of the distribution of political power in Germany to know what were the wishes of the General Staff and the Naval Staff for the strategic defence of the country. The leading generals were of the opinion that the industrial districts in western Germany bordered too nearly upon the existing German frontier; that a strip of French territory must be taken in order to safeguard the industrial districts in German Lorraine; and that for the defence of the Rhineland at least Liège should become German. It would be still better were Belgium to remain under the protection of Germany. In the east they desired a readjustment of the frontier that would afford better protection to Upper Silesia, east and west Prussia, involving a cession of Russo-Polish territory. It is clear that the war aims of the General Staff largely coincided with those of the industrialists; for Longwy-Briey lay within the territory which the generals demanded for the protection of Lorraine while soldiers and industrialists were at one in their views in regard to Belgium. The Navy also demanded that Germany should retain Belgium for so long as Germany was in possession of the coast of Flanders she could hold England in check by means of submarines.

Out of all these different war aims there was created a unified programme for the so-called German "peace of conquest" of which the vocal protagonists were the members of the Pan-German Association. The enthusiasm with which the governing class in Germany took up this idea is not to be explained on the ground of personal interest alone. The political brains among the Prussian aristocracy and the industrialists recognized that in any event the war must result in a grave threat to their own power and to the old governmental system in Germany. In event of an unsuccessful conclusion to the war a terrible disaster was to be expected. If, on the other hand, the war ended with a peace

on the *status quo ante* basis, the German nation would be compelled to pay thousands of millions in war expenses without having derived any advantage. These millions could only be raised
by the imposition of heavy taxes. On their return from the Front
the soldiers would find, after all their sacrifices, an impoverished
country awaiting them and a Government which required from
them the payment of huge taxes. All this would arouse such a
feeling in the people that a revolution would be inevitable. According to the so-called "Annexationists" the old system could
only survive in Germany were the State in a position at the end
of the war to offer the nation a definite compensation for its
sacrifices: either reparations from the enemy, or land for colonization, or greater scope for industrial expansion, or, best of all,
all these together.

Hence the Conservatives and the majority of the National
Liberals saw in a German victory the last hope of salvation for
the old Germany. Although they did not know the real gravity
of the situation, they must nevertheless have often said to themselves during 1915–16 that a complete military victory on the
part of Germany over all her enemies was not very probable. At
this juncture the Navy spread a rumour abroad that it was in
possession of a weapon which would compel Germany's chief
enemy, England, to listen to reason within six months. This
weapon was a ruthless submarine campaign. An exaggerated regard for English and American susceptibilities made Bethmann-
Hollweg reluctant to permit the use of this decisive instrument.
The "procrastinators" at Court, men like the chiefs of the Emperor's naval and military secretariats, von Valentini and von
Müller, proved themselves Bethmann-Hollweg's most efficient
allies in this regard. But the officers, Prussian *Junkers,* and industrialists argued as follows:

"war is permeating the country with its poison, eating away the
roots of German power, and strengthening socialism and democracy; unrestricted submarine warfare must be brought into
operation without regard for anybody's feelings; and Bethmann-
Hollweg removed from his post. Thus, and thus only, can Germany prove herself victorious and achieve a victorious peace.
Thus, and thus only, can the revolution be avoided and the traditional governmental system survive."

The war aims of the Social Democratic workmen were utterly opposed to those of the governing class. For reasons already mentioned above the working class was filled with the deepest suspicion of its rulers and with the determination to end the war as speedily as possible. The masses of the populace gained the impression that the war was not unwelcome to the higher Staff Officers and the great industrialists. They learnt that their rulers were hatching great schemes of conquest, and they were indoctrinated with the official optimistic accounts of the situation on the several Fronts. The enemy offensives had been thrown back at all points and not an enemy foot stood upon German soil. Was it not possible, then, so the workmen thought to themselves, to conclude a peace by compromise and without conquests? Were not these schemes of conquest on the part of the governing class the real obstacle to peace? The Social Democratic workmen saw their suspicions justified in the declarations of the Conservatives and Pan-Germans that Germany dare not content herself with a peace by compromise and must fight to the end for a victorious peace. It seemed to the workmen that the very men by whom they were held down in political and economic life and in the army alike were also responsible for the prolongation of the war. It was these men who had to be deprived of power in order to make an end to the general suffering. It was thus that the battle-cry "Down with the Pan-Germans and Annexationists" awoke the spirit of class-warfare in the working man. With this battle-cry the proletariate burst the bonds of the *Burgfrieden* and began once more the fight for political power. In the eyes of the Social Democratic working class the Annexationists were synonymous with the governing class of Imperial Germany. The overthrow of the Annexationists thus meant the domination of the Social Democrats in Germany.

The passionate refusal of the workers to tolerate any form of annexation created a difficult problem for the leaders of the Social Democratic Party to solve. Although the Party had not taken up an independent political attitude in the sense desired by Engels, it had nevertheless held firmly to the tradition handed down to it from Marx and Engels that the chief aim of the war should be the destruction of the Tsardom. The Party agreed that a German victory in the east should be used to liberate all the peoples, and especially the Poles, living under Russian tyranny.

At the same time it should have been perfectly clear to them that an Imperial and aristocratic Germany could not play the role of liberator to the nations subject to Russia. A Poland, Lithuania, and Courland that had been "liberated" through a victory of the Imperial armies could never be anything else than the vassals of the German aristocrats and industrialists. In adopting for the west the formula "no annexations and a peace on the basis of the *status quo,*" the Social Democrats must have been prepared to see the same principle extended to the east. In order, however, to avoid the abandonment of the war with Tsardom that had been one of their proclaimed war aims on August 4, 1914, the Social Democrats were forced to act in an illogical manner. They opposed all plans for a public or secret policy of annexations in Belgium and northern France, while at the same time they raised no serious objections to the creation by Germany at the cost of Russia of new States out of Courland, Poland, and Lithuania. It is true that the Social Democrats demanded that in these "liberated" countries the right of self-determination should be put into practice; a right that was valueless from the standpoint of practical politics.

It is worthy of emphasis that the German working class pursued with a special hatred any one who proclaimed himself to be in favour of the annexation of Belgium, and especially of the Flanders coast, while they made no opposition to proposals for annexations in the east. The truth is that the mass of the population was not indisposed to an extension of German territory and power, but only to a policy of annexation that would prolong the war. This attitude on their part appears quite natural if considered as a whole. Why should the working class look upon the political frontiers of Europe as they existed in July 1914 as sacrosanct? These frontiers were only the result of a thousand diplomatic accidents. What the working class did oppose with all their might was the prolongation of the miseries attendant upon the war merely in order—as it appeared to them—that a few industrialists might profit in Belgium. The vast majority of the German populace looked upon Russia as already defeated. The strongest and most dangerous enemies of Germany seemed in their eyes to be England and France, to whom concessions must be made in order to achieve a peace. England had declared that she had entered the war in defence of Belgium, and that the complete restoration of Belgium was her cardinal object in prosecuting the war. It was clear, therefore, that Germany must give up Belgium, and that the Annexationists who sought to hinder that being done must be deprived of their power. From a psychological standpoint this attitude on the part of the German working class is thoroughly comprehensible. Yet from an objective standpoint it was mistaken: the way to the speedy conclusion of peace lay not through concessions to England but in an understanding with Russia.

The question of war aims broke up the unity of the Centre. The Conservative leaders wished to unite with the Parties of the Right while the Christian Trade Unions were no less desirous than were the Social Democrats of a peace by understanding. Although the business communities in the great cities had no objection to an extension of German territory and influence, yet they desired it to be carried out along the line which was likely to arouse the least opposition, namely, by the creation of new States in the East and by the completion of the Berlin-Baghdad scheme. They further hoped that the Quadruple Alliance of Germany, Austria-Hungary, Bulgaria and Turkey would result in a permanent politico-economic alliance in which their allies would follow the leadership of Germany. This scheme, of which the protagonist was the Progressive leader, Friedrich Neumann, was altogether Utopian, inasmuch as neither the Habsburg Monarchy nor the Balkan States nor Turkey were prepared to submit to the hegemony of Germany.

Such was the great scheme of annexation that came into being in Germany during the war. If it had been carried out, it would have resulted in the political and economic subjection of foreign States with almost a hundred million inhabitants to Germany. As such it was seen in its true light by English and American statesmen. Within Germany itself, however, it aroused less feeling than might have been expected, since the proletariate in thinking of annexations had in mind only the plans of the industrialists and the General Staff with regard to Belgium and northern France, while the commercial classes and the Progressives showed no interest whatever in the more particular war aims of the industrialists. The majority of the peasants, like the workmen, hoped for a speedy ending to the war without troubling to formulate any special conditions.

The controversy as to war aims which steadily intensified during 1915–16, was especially unwelcome to Bethmann-Hollweg, since it compelled the Government to abandon its reserve and to define its attitude towards the question at issue; and such a proceeding was regarded by Bethmann-Hollweg as an infringement of the *Burgfrieden*. He sought to make use of the censorship in order to divert the people from this controversy with the result that the evil he sought to prevent only became worse. For all classes in the population were at least united in the desire to know whither the war was leading them and for what object it was being fought. Bethmann-Hollweg's tactics only had the effect of driving the discussion beneath the surface with the result of making agreement between the controversialists still more difficult of attainment. The Chancellor himself regarded the situation in which Germany found herself as grave and almost hopeless. The Chief of the General Staff, von Falkenhayn, was in the main of his opinion. If Bethmann-Hollweg had only published an official and accurate statement, covered by the authority of the General Staff as to the nature of the military situation, he could have destroyed the annexationist propaganda in Germany at a single stroke. That he did not do so was due to his fear lest any such action might have the effect of weakening the endurance of the nation. Instead of coming before the nation with a clearly defined plan for the further conduct of the war, and with a precise programme of the terms on which Germany was prepared to conclude peace, Bethmann-Hollweg took refuge in evasions from a desire to avoid hurting the susceptibilities of the Conservatives and National Liberals. At the same time his speeches were of such a nature that the Social Democrats were able to interpret them in a sense favourable to their own plans. His programme came in the end to be a compound of the demands of both parties. By conceding each a part of its demands the Chancellor thought he would be able to restore unity within the nation and to allay the domestic strife, and it was only in the East that he came forward with a pronounced policy.

As early as August 19, 1915, Bethmann-Hollweg announced in the Reichstag, in words that left little room for doubt in the minds of his hearers, that Germany would not restore Poland to Russia. His statement was the consequence of the German victories over the Russians in the spring and summer months of that year. On April 5, 1916, the Chancellor distinctly told the Reich-

stag that the "liberated" Poles, Letts, Lithuanians, and Balts
would never again be permitted to come under Russian rule.
Bethmann-Hollweg thus thought to meet the demands of the
Social Democrats at the same moment as he satisfied those of
the General Staff and the Agrarians. Since her defeat in 1915
Russia had been virtually isolated from her allies, and she bore
the chief burden of the war to the accompaniment of a steadily
increasing threat of revolution. Since the German victories in
the east had not proved decisive in a military sense, it was all the
more important for Germany to derive what political benefit
she could from those victories. It is probable that Germany could
have concluded a separate peace with Russia on the basis of the
status quo in the autumn of 1915 and throughout 1916. When,
however, Bethmann-Hollweg announced to the Russian Government that Russia must be prepared in all circumstances to lose
her Baltic provinces, the Tsar naturally preferred to remain loyal
to his allies.

In the west Bethmann-Hollweg was determined upon the acquisition of Longwy-Briey, while at the same time he was prepared
to compensate the French by a rectification of the frontier in
other districts of Alsace-Lorraine. It was obvious that France
would not surrender her valuable iron-mines before she had
suffered a complete military defeat. Any proposal to compensate
the French in other ways for the loss of these mines could not
be taken seriously. Bethmann-Hollweg indeed made no public
pronouncement on this subject. Instead he touched in his speech
in the Reichstag on April 5, 1916, on the subject of the future of
Belgium. He assured the Reichstag that the pre-war guarantee of
Belgium's neutrality was a thing of the past, and that Germany
must be given sufficient guarantees that Belgium would not in
future become a vassal-State under Anglo-French domination. He
added that it was the duty of Germany to protect the national
traditions and language of the Flemish inhabitants of Belgium.
This amounted in fact to an endorsement of the Pan-German
programme for a German protectorate over Belgium. Bethmann-
Hollweg even went so far as to intimate his agreement with the
proposals in regard to Belgium which were based upon the support of the Flemings in opposition to the French-speaking Wal-
loons. These proposals were founded upon a grave politico-historical misunderstanding. The two nationalities included within

the Belgian State stood to one another in the same relationship as the French-speaking to the German-speaking Swiss. Here there could be no question of "liberation." At least ninety-nine per cent of the Flemish people looked with hostility upon any interference on the part of Germany in Belgian affairs. If Germany had succeeded in calling into being an autonomous Flanders, she would have only been able to maintain it in existence by the exercise of military force.

Although it is easy to understand the fears entertained by the German Government lest England might make of Belgium a jumping-off ground for her continental schemes, yet nevertheless this danger was only to be met by means of an agreement between Germany, France, and Russia. If Germany had showed that she really had the defence of the European Continent at heart, then she could have demanded guarantees from Belgium (an entire Belgium and not the Utopian Flanders) that she would place herself in the ranks of a European coalition. When, however, Bethmann-Hollweg contemplated war aims whose attainment could only be possible after a complete defeat of France and Russia, how did he then propose to get his own way in the Belgian question against the opposition of England? Still more—how could he reconcile such a programme with his pessimistic outlook on the war?

It is quite clear that Bethmann-Hollweg drew up his programme without reference to the military and international situation in which Germany found herself, and that he intended it to serve as a compromise in domestic politics. Although in regard to German war aims in the west Bethmann-Hollweg was virtually in agreement with the views of the Conservatives and National Liberals, yet at the same time he chose his words so carefully that he avoided giving offence to the Social Democrats. It was even possible to interpret his words to mean that he desired no conquests but simply a peace by understanding. Yet his cautiousness only resulted in enraging the Conservatives and National Liberals. Although Bethmann-Hollweg actually offered the Annexationists all that they asked for, they were not content in that they desired that the German war aims should be publicly and resolutely announced to the nation as a test of the Government's authority within the country. Moreover, they wished to render it impossible for Scheidemann to say that he had placed the right interpretation upon the Chancellor's words. The governing class in Germany was in truth not even willing to let it appear that the Social Democrats exerted any influence upon the conduct of the war. The whole question of war aims was primarily a domestic issue for both the Pan-Germans and the proletariate. . . .

24   FROM   *John W. Wheeler-Bennett*
Brest-Litovsk, the Forgotten Peace, March 1918

The activities of Adolf Hitler gave Germany's World War I war aims new significance and importance even before the actual outbreak of World War II. This is evident from the important study of Brest-Litovsk by the English historian, John W. Wheeler-Bennett, who is most famous for his studies of Hindenburg and the German army.

INTRODUCTION

Twenty years ago, on March 3, 1918, the first treaty of peace between belligerent parties in the World War was signed by the Central Powers and Russia at Brest-Litovsk. Few at that time appreciated its full significance, and, in the later years, when events crowded hard upon each other, the Peace of Brest-Litovsk was forgotten.

Yet, this Peace of Brest-Litovsk is one of the important mile-stones in modern history, for with its signature begins a chain of events which leads directly to the happenings of to-day; a chain which numbers among its links some of the greatest incidents in war and peace. The Treaty of Brest-Litovsk not only signified the apparently complete victory of German arms in the East, and the greatest diplomatic and military humiliation which

SOURCE (24). Reprinted from John W. Wheeler-Bennett, *Brest-Litovsk. The Forgotten Peace. March 1918,* with the permission of St. Martin's Press, Inc. Macmillan & Co., Ltd., pp. xi–xvii, 269–275, 304–308.

Russia had ever sustained in a long history of defeat, but, with the exception of the Treaty of Versailles, it had consequences and repercussions more vitally important than any other peace settlement since the Congress of Vienna.

It was the course of the negotiations at Brest-Litovsk which prompted President Wilson to promulgate his famous Fourteen Points, in an attempt to keep the Russians from concluding a separate peace. The rapacity of the victor's terms imposed upon Russia disclosed to the rest of the world the domination which the Supreme Command had attained in Germany, and the impossibility of arriving at a "peace of understanding" with a Germany in the hands of such rulers. The realization of this fact produced that final unity of purpose between the United States of America and the Western Powers, that implacable "will to victory," which all previous negotiations had failed to achieve, and which assured the ultimate defeat of Germany.

The Peace of Brest-Litovsk preserved Bolshevism. Its conclusion provided Lenin with the essential "breathing-space" for consolidating the Russian Revolution against the attempts to overthrow it from within. At the same time, the treaty marks the beginning of that infiltration of active Communism into Germany which materially contributed to her collapse some nine months later. For, with the opening of the negotiations, there emerged that new and potent factor in world diplomacy, Bolshevik propaganda; propaganda carried on by the party which formed the Government of the Soviet State, but of whose activities that Government professed official ignorance. "The Party does not sign the treaty," said Lenin, "and for the Party the Government is not responsible." It was upon this policy of "parallel diplomacy," first used at Brest, that the activities of the Third International were based after its organization in 1919.

Such were the more immediate results of Brest-Litovsk, but its influence is still discernible in the political life and ideological trends of both Russia and Germany to-day. The psychology of Brest-Litovsk is still strong in both countries, though with strangely different manifestations, and is responsible both for the genesis of the Nazi ambitions for hegemony over Eastern and South-Eastern Europe, and, in some degree possibly, for the actions of those leading members of the Old Bolshevik Party which have recently ended in their own destruction.

• • •

The Weimar Republic, with the support of the majority opinion on the German General Staff, represented by General von Seeckt, sought to reach a *rapprochement* with the Soviet Union, and largely succeeded in doing so by the Treaty of Rapallo and the Military Agreement of April 3, 1922, and the German-Russian Non-Aggression Treaty of 1926. There remained, however, a minority who followed in the Hoffmann tradition, regarding Bolshevism as the root of all evil, and dreaming of the ultimate realization of those far-reaching plans for German expansion in Eastern Europe which so sadly eluded them after Brest-Litovsk.

Added to this is the very definite view which Adolf Hitler himself holds regarding the treaty, and which the National Socialist Party has sedulously fostered into a legend and an attainable ideal. For the ideology which actuated the dictation of the treaty has not been replaced by any other set of ideas, and has become the conviction of a large part of the German people. The present German generation—the generation of Nazi Germany—regards the principles of Brest-Litovsk and the motives lying behind it as an actual political programme.[1] None has been more eloquent in this view than the Führer himself, in his comparison of the treaty with the Peace of Versailles. "I placed the two Treaties side by side, compared them point by point, showed the positively boundless humanity of the one in contrast to the inhuman cruelty of the other," he wrote in *Mein Kampf*. "In those days I spoke on this subject before audiences of 2000 at which I was often exposed to the gaze of 3600 hostile eyes. And three hours later I had before me a surging mass filled with righteous indignation and boundless wrath."[2] With this as a pointer it is not surprising to find Hitler stating somewhat later in his work: "We [the National Socialists] stop the perpetual migration towards the south and west of Europe and fix our gaze on the land in the East . . . when we talk of new lands in Europe, we are bound to think first of Russia and her border States."[3] And again: "We must not forget that the international Jew, who continues to dominate Russia, does not regard Germany as an ally, but as a State des-

---

[1] Cf. "Germany's Present Eastern Policy and the Lessons of Brest-Litovsk", by "Pragmaticus", *Slavonic and Eastern European Review*, xv. No. 44.

[2] Adolf Hitler, *Mein Kampf* (Munich, 1938), i. 523–525.

[3] *Ibid*. ii. 742.

tined to undergo a similar fate. The menace which Russia suffered under is one which perpetually hangs over Germany; Germany is the next great objective of Bolshevism."[4]

Here then is combined in one political philosophy the doctrine of pre-war Pan-Germanism, the all-pervading hatred of the Jew, and the ideological opposition to Bolshevism, and the only means by which this philosophy may be given practical application is through a reversion to the German mentality of Brest-Litovsk. It is not unimportant that political writers of 1917 talked as freely of German equality (*Gleichberechtigung*) as do the Nazi pundits to-day, but they were more frank in their interpretation of it. "The issue between us and England constitutes not so much isolated problems as the conflict between England's world domination hitherto and our endeavor to obtain *Gleichberechtigung* in the world. That is why the war is being waged," wrote Professor Hettner in his book, *Der deutsche Frieden und die deutsche Zukunft*; and years later Hitler epitomised this statement in a single sentence: "Germany will be a World Power or nothing at all." He admits that England will not tolerate Germany as a World Power, but says that this is not for the moment an urgent question, for Germany is first concerned with uniting the German race and fighting for territory in Europe.[1]

Reverting to the Ludendorff thesis that "German prestige demands that we should hold a strong protecting hand, not only over German citizens but over *all* Germans," Hitler aims first at the realization of a *Deutschtum* stretching from Jutland to the Brenner and from Strasburg to Riga, and later at securing for Germany enough territory to accommodate 200,000,000 Germans. This expansion, according to the views expressed in *Mein Kampf*, the undisputed Bible of the Third Reich, is to take place in the east and south-east of Europe, in those territories to which German colonization during the Middle Ages was directed— "We begin again where we left off six centuries ago"—and to the Ukraine and Southern Russia as a whole.

Read in this light the attitude assumed by Nazi Germany towards Austria and Czechoslovakia, towards the Baltic States and Poland, and towards Hungary and Rumania takes on a new

---

[4] *Ibid.* pp. 750–751.
[1] Hitler, *Mein Kampf*, ii. 699.

significance. The expansion of Germany thus conceived envisages the readjustment of existing conditions in Central and Eastern Europe corresponding to the political system which the Pan-German Party and the Supreme Command planned during the war, the skeleton structure of which was completed under the Treaties of Brest-Litovsk and Bucharest; that is to say, the political hegemony of Germany over all remotely Germanic States and a mediated acquisition of Russian territory. The methods employed differ in each case. Austria was first terrorised and then annexed to the German Reich. Czechoslovakia is subjected to threats and propaganda calculated to stimulate "spontaneous revolt." Poland and the Baltic States, as in the days of Brest-Litovsk, are offered compromises and the expectation of security— though it may be recalled that in *Mein Kampf* the Poles are not only dismissed as "inferior," but Polish children are classed on the same low level as Jews, negroes, and Asiatics. Towards Hungary, Yugoslavia, and Rumania a policy of blandishment and flattery is adopted in the hope of winning away the first from Italian, and the two latter from French influence.

• • •

An examination of the instruments signed at Brest-Litovsk on March 3 indicates the haste with which the peace terms were finally drawn up. The chief anxiety of the German General Staff was to conclude a formal settlement with Russia and to turn their attention to their great offensive on the Western Front. This was the gambler's last throw on which he had staked all; if the battle were won and the Allies sufficiently defeated to discuss peace, the Germans could take up the matter of their eastern acquisitions at their leisure; while if the battle were lost, they might still find a possibility of exploiting Russia. The matter of immediate importance was that they had successfully broken through the steel ring with which the Allied blockade had encircled Germany, and were no longer in danger of defeat by starvation. The very fact of freedom from any military threat in the East was a sufficient "interim dividend," provided that the ordinary commercial relations were re-established.

It is for this reason that the economic and commercial agreements signed at Brest-Litovsk appear at first sight to be less harsh than the political sections of the treaties. Germany, having

staked out her claim to territorial aggrandizement by the simple
process of declaring that certain extensive areas under her occupation were no longer part of the Russian State, could afford to
wait until the issue in the West had been decided, before going
more deeply into the problem of how best to exploit the rich
treasures which now lay open to her. With the Allies safely
disposed of, the political and territorial settlement of the vast
regions which Germany now controlled could be shaped to pay
the cost of the three and a half years of war. Such, at least, was
the reasoning of the Supreme Command at the moment the
treaty was signed. Moreover, having already reached a seemingly
satisfactory agreement with the Ukraine whereby the rich lands
of south-western Russia passed under their control, they could,
for the time being, afford to hold their hand in the development
of their plans for the economic exploitation of Great Russia.

But the political clauses of the treaty could scarcely be excelled
in Draconian severity. Since Bulgaria had never been, and
Austria-Hungary had ceased to be a territorial neighbour of
Russia, the cessions of territory were made to Germany and
Turkey. The much discussed fate of Poland, Courland, and
Lithuania was disposed of in Article 3: "The territories lying to
the west of the line agreed upon by the contracting parties, which
formerly belonged to Russia, will no longer be subject to Russian sovereignty. . . . Germany and Austria-Hungary purpose to
determine the future status of these territories in agreement with
their populations."[1] Thus the fiction of self-determination was
maintained. Moreover, by Article 6, Russia recognized the
Ukrainian treaty with the Central Powers, and therefore also the
independence of the Ukraine from the Russian Republic. All
Ukrainian territory, together with Estonia and Livonia, was to
be evacuated by the Russians, the latter to be occupied by a
German police force "until security is ensured by proper national
institutions and until public order has been established." Finland[2] and the Aaland Islands were also, under the same article,

[1] *Texts of the Russian "Peace"*, pp. 15–16.

[2] The independence of Finland had been recognized by the Soviet Government in December 1917, and Red Guards had been sent to assist in the
formation of a "Finnish Socialist Republic of Workmen." With this Government the Bolsheviks signed their first international treaty, ironically enough
on March 1, at which time the Reds had been driven out of Helsingfors by

to be cleared of Russian troops, and the islands were to be permanently neutralized under an agreement between Germany,
Russia, Sweden, and Finland.[1] The Russian army was to be completely demobilized and the navy, together with any Allied war-
ships which might be in Russian waters, either disarmed immediately or detained in Russian ports until the conclusion of a
general peace (Article 5).[2] When this process of disarmament had
been completed and a general peace concluded, the Germans
graciously agreed to evacuate all the remaining Russian territory
occupied by them for which provision had not already been
made in the treaty (Article 4).[3]

By the same article Russia promised to "ensure the immediate
evacuation of the provinces of Eastern Anatolia and their lawful
return to Turkey," and likewise of the Sanjaks of Ardahan, Kars,
and Batum, which were to determine their own future status "in
agreement with the neighbouring States, especially Turkey."
(Again the Banquo ghost of self-determination at the feast!) A
supplementary agreement between Russia and Turkey regulated
the execution of this provision, and by it Russia was forbidden
to concentrate more than one division, even for drill purposes,
on the borders of the three Sanjaks or in Caucasia without previous notice to the Central Powers, until the conclusion of a general
peace. On the other hand, Turkey was permitted to keep her
army on a war footing.[4] The importance of this retrocession of
the three Sanjaks—for they had been annexed by Russia in 1878
as a reprisal for the nonfulfilment of treaty obligations—lay not
so much in the return to Turkey of the great fortress of Kars,
which in past wars had been the Verdun of the Caucasus, but in

---

the Whites, with German assistance. The only point of interest in this agreement—which was legally as valueless, at that moment, as the treaty signed
between the Central Powers and the Ukrainian *Rada*—was the provision that
all disputes arising out of it should be settled by an arbitration court of
which the president should be appointed by "the administration of the
Democratic Socialist Party of the Swedish Left, except if otherwise stipulated."
On March 7 an elaborate treaty of peace, with commercial provisions, was
signed between the Central Powers and the Whites. (See *Texts of the Finland
"Peace,"* U.S. Department of State, Washington, D.C., 1918.)

1 *Texts of the Russian "Peace,"* pp. 17–18.

2 *Ibid.* pp. 16–17.

3 *Ibid.* p. 16.

4 *Ibid.* pp. 167–171.

the fact that Batum was the key and the port of the rich oilfields of Baku and Azerbaizhan, which thus lay open to the exploitation of the Central Powers.

The formula of "no indemnities" was adhered to theoretically in Article 9 of the Russian treaty whereby the Central Powers waived all claims to compensation for war costs and reparation payments, but these materialized in a disguised form under Article 8 (and Article 16 of the Legal-Political Treaty), which regulated the exchange of prisoners of war.[1] By this provision "each contracting party will reimburse the expenses incurred by the other party for its nationals who have been made prisoners of war." Now the number of Russians captured by the Germans and Austrians was considerably larger than those taken by the Russians from the Central Powers, particularly if from the latter were subtracted those Czechs who were being formed by Dr. Masaryk into legions to fight against Germany. The burden which would fall upon Russia under this provision would therefore be considerably heavier than the costs incurred by the Central Powers. They had protested during the negotiations against its inclusion, arguing that the employment of prisoners of war at low wages led to profits which exceeded the expense of their maintenance.[2] According to Russian computations the sum payable by Russia under this arrangement would amount to between four and five milliards of gold roubles, but the Germans swept the estimate aside as "a great exaggeration" and the provision stood in the treaty.[3] So much for "no indemnities."

The commercial agreements annexed to the general treaty[4] did

---

[1] *Texts of the Russian "Peace"*, pp. 19, 127.

[2] Nor was this provision universally popular in Germany. On the publication of the peace treaty the German agrarian press was filled with letters from Junker landlords, protesting against the exchange of Russian prisoners of war on grounds that, without their assistance, German agriculture would suffer an inevitable catastrophe. Some writers suggested the postponement of exchange till September, when the harvesting would be over; others proposed that the entire male population of the occupied territories ceded by Russia should be transported to Germany in order to furnish cheap agricultural labour.

[3] Gratz and Schüller, p. 119.

[4] *Texts of the Russian "Peace"*, pp. 25–28.

not renew Russia's former commercial treaties with Germany (1904) and with Austria-Hungary (1906), but they maintained the Russian tariff of 1903, even in cases not provided for in the pre-war treaties, while the Central Powers in this respect kept a free hand. The Germans had wished to keep the treaty of 1904 in force until the end of 1930, though with a number of amendments in favour of Germany, but the Russians were opposed to this[1] and the Austrians but half-hearted in support of their allies.[2] Therefore, because time pressed and the Germans believed that they would have plenty of opportunity later to arrive at a favourable commercial arrangement with Russia, a provisional agreement was concluded which should stand until the conclusion of a general peace, or at any rate till the end of 1919. In the meantime each country was to enjoy most-favoured-nation treatment in the territory of the other, but Russia was not to prohibit the export of, nor to levy an export tax on, lumber or ores (Clause 3). Apart from this restriction, the agreement was entirely reciprocal, and Russia was allowed to retain certain unilateral privileges such as the right to tax foreign commercial travellers, while Russian commercial travellers in Germany and Austria-Hungary remained untaxed. The magnanimity of this concession may be gauged from the obvious lack of opportunities for Russia to exercise this right.

Finally, there was the important provision contained in Article 2 of the general treaty, the prohibition of propaganda.[3] All the contracting parties undertook reciprocally to refrain from any agitation or propaganda against each other's Government or public or military institutions, and a special obligation devolved upon Russia to extend this prohibition to the territories occupied by the Central Powers. By this flimsy formula did Germany hope to protect herself against contagion from the effects of the virus which she herself had introduced into Russia. How lightly this

---

[1] The German-Russian tariff treaty was originally negotiated in 1894 after a tariff war in which Russia was defeated. In 1904, owing to the Russian defeats in Manchuria and the incipient revolution, the Germans succeeded in negotiating a renewal of the treaty on terms still more advantageous to themselves.

[2] Gratz and Schüller, p. 122.

[3] *Texts of the Russian "Peace"*, p. 15.

undertaking rested upon the Soviet authorities may be guessed by the promises which Lenin had already made to the Petrograd Soviet.

These, then, were the provisions of the Treaty of Brest-Litovsk. At one stroke Germany had extended her control of Eastern Europe to the Arctic Ocean and the Black Sea, and had acquired the undisputed arbitrament of the fate of fifty-five million inhabitants of Russia's western fringe—so much for the doctrines of "no annexation" and "self-determination"; while by the agreements with Rumania (signed on March 5)[1] and with the Ukraine, and the Turkish agreement with Russia, she had gained access to vast resources of wheat and petroleum. Such was the prospect unfolded before the avid eyes of the Supreme Command; such was the price which Lenin paid for the salvation of the Russian Revolution. . . .

It was in almost festive mood that the Reichstag interrupted its scheduled order of the day on March 18 to begin discussion of the Brest-Litovsk treaty. The parties of the Right and Centre were openly jubilant at having achieved peace in the East on their own terms, and expressed enthusiastic hopes that the great offensive in the West, which was about to be launched, would shortly result in a similar peace with the remainder of the Allied and Associated Powers. The parties of the Left were critical in a varying degree, but only the Independent Socialists appeared to have the courage of their convictions.

The formal case for ratification was put by the Chancellor and the Under-Secretary of State for Foreign Affairs, von dem Bussche, who defended the peace terms as a whole, as containing "no conditions whatever dishonouring to Russia, no mention of oppressive war indemnities, and no forcible appropriation of Russian territories." The old fiction of the self-determination of Courland and Lithuania was repeated, while in respect of the other occupied territories Hertling stated expressly: "We are not thinking of establishing ourselves permanently [*uns festsetzen*] in Estonia or Livonia, we wish only to live on good friendly terms after the war with the political forces which are coming into existence

---

[1] *Texts of the Rumanian "Peace"* (U.S. Department of State, Washington, D.C., 1918), pp. 3–6.

there, in such a way that will not exclude peace and friendly relations with Russia."[1]

That this was not the view or intention of the Supreme Command was made clear by the words of their usual mouthpiece,
Gustav Stresemann, who viewed with apprehension the proposal
to separate Courland, with Riga, from Livonia and Estonia.
"Here the right of self-determination does not apply!" cried the
man who was later to lead Germany to Geneva, and added, "I do
not believe in Wilson's universal league of nations; I believe that
after the conclusion of peace it will burst like a soap-bubble."[2]

Scheidemann, in a speech lacking his usual fire, decried the
treaty as not being a peace of understanding and therefore incompatible with the Peace Resolution of July 1917,[1] to which Grober,
the Democrat leader, replied that it was not a question of whether
it was or was not a peace of understanding, but whether a peace
treaty could have been obtained in any other way. This question
he himself answered in the negative, adding somewhat inconse-
quently, "We have every reason to ask in all humility where we
should have been without the merciful help of God." At which
the deputies of the Centre gave "lively applause."[2]

The real opposition to the treaty was voiced by the Social
Democrat, David, and the Independent Socialist leader, Haase,
who spared no one in their attacks. "My party has only one feeling, that of shame that a peace of the sword should have been
ruthlessly forced upon our eastern neighbours," cried Haase.
"Things in the East have been arranged in accordance with the
mad wishes of the annexationist politicians."[3] At Brest-Litovsk
not only the Bolsheviks but also our own diplomatists have given

[1] *Verhandlungen des Reichstags,* March 18, 1918, pp. 4425–4427.

[2] *Ibid.* March 19, 1918, pp. 4453, 4462. How accurately Stresemann inter-
preted the view of the General Staff may be judged from the fact that on
April 9, at the opening of the Estonian Diet, the German Commanding
General, Freiherr von Seckendorff, announced that "German troops will not
leave Estonia; they will stay here for permanent protection" (*Texts of the
Russian "Peace",* p. 225).

[1] *Verhandlungen des Reichstags,* March 22, 1918, p. 4536.

[2] *Ibid.* March 22, 1918, pp. 4636–4639.

[3] *Ibid.* March 22, 1918, pp. 4540–4544.

in to the representatives of armed force," corroborated David.[4] Together they laid bare, amidst the enraged interruptions of the Right and the nervous embarrassment of the official Social Democrat *Fraktion,* the pusillanimity and hypocrisy of the governmental policy during the negotiations. Together they flayed the jingo policies of the High Command and the *Vaterlandspartei,* and in conclusion David struck at the sacred caste of privilege itself. "A peace resting on the power of the sword is the weakest peace known. Germany cannot solve the problem presented in its general policy by the methods and ways of the old Prussian ruling class. Peace at home, peace abroad can be won only through right and freedom."

But the result of the debate had always been a foregone conclusion. It mattered little to the Reichstag that Clemenceau had written on behalf of the Allies: "Peace treaties such as these we do not and cannot acknowledge. Our own ends are very different; we are fighting, and mean to continue fighting, in order to finish once for all with this policy of plunder."[1] What did matter was that while the debate was proceeding the *Kaiserschlacht* had made its brilliant opening, and that when the final vote was taken, the British Fifth Army was reeling back in retreat before the hammer-blows of Ludendorff.

With the news of victory in their ears, the deputies ratified the treaty on March 22. Only the Independent Socialists opposed. The Social Democrats abstained from voting and thereby forfeited their right of protest when later they themselves were forced to submit to a dictated peace. Lacking the moral courage to oppose that which they had publicly declared to be wrong, they displayed both that lack of political flair and that infirmity of purpose which was to bring them to destruction some fifteen years later.[2]

---

[4] *Ibid.* March 18, 1918, pp. 4431–4440.

[1] Cumming and Pettit, pp. 92–94.

[2] The effect of Brest-Litovsk upon the psychology of the Social Democrats was peculiar in every way. They opposed the treaty in debate but refused to vote against its ratification. They were deeply perturbed by the storm of protest which arose from the outside world, yet they continued until the breakdown in October and November to follow the dictates of the High Command. Finally, they were so greatly impressed by the rapidity with which

The remainder of the deputies was swept forward on the wave of military success, with the false dawn of victory before their eyes. The might of German arms had achieved so much, it must now triumph completely. The good sword which had brought them peace in the East would also hack its way to peace in the West. They voted with the sublime faith of dupes. Yet, even in this moment of ephemeral triumph, there could almost be heard the voice of Nemesis crying through the Chamber the gibe that Radek had hurled into the indignant face of Hoffmann, "It is your day now, but in the end the Allies will put a Brest-Litovsk treaty upon you."

Russia had got rid of a "victor's peace" that they placed their signatures to the Treaty of Versailles in the sublime hope that the public opinion of the world would demand a revision of its terms within a very short time. It took twenty years and cost the Social Democratic Party its life before the treaty was revised—unilaterally.

PART TWO

Post-1945 Documents and Interpretations

A. The Sources

25 FROM   *The Role of the Interest Groups: Meeting of the Subcommittee on War Aims of the German Industry War Committee (Kriegsausschuss der deutschen Industrie), November 7, 1914*

Historians have become more interested in the role played by pressure groups in influencing foreign policy and in the relationship between domestic politics and foreign affairs. The document below is particularly interesting because it demonstrates how new evidence may confirm or reinforce old hypotheses and, at the same time, raise new questions. The statement by Alfred Hugenberg, a director of Krupp and a notorious Pan-German and right wing politician, is very explicit evidence of how conservatives hoped to use annexations to fight domestic sociopolitical reform. The remarks of Gustav Stresemann, a leader of the National Liberal Party and the Foreign Minister of the Weimar Republic from 1924 to 1929, show that not all businessmen shared Hugenberg's view of the relationship between domestic reforms and imperialism. Furthermore, the remarks of Carl Friedrich von Siemens, the head of the great electrotechnical corporation which bears his name, suggest that

SOURCE (25). Translated by the editor from "Aufzeichnung über die Sitzung des Unterausschusses des Kriegsausschusses der deutschen Industrie am 7. November 1914," Nachlass Gustav Stresemann, Reel 6839, Frames H16925–H126927 (microfilmed by the U.S. National Archives).

*not all businessmen were equally imperialistic. Thus, the new
evidence provided by this document supports previously held
arguments concerning the annexationism of the business community and the use of annexationism to fight domestic reform,
but it also suggests that some differentiation is necessary. Heavy
industry (coal, iron, steel) seems to have been most annexationist and reactionary. The textile industry, which Stresemann frequently represented, and the electrotechnical industry held more
moderate views.*

It was stressed by all that considerations of military security
would make the occupation of Antwerp, Calais and Ostend, as
well as the annexation of the French fortified territory a necessity. By contrast opinions were very divided as to whether or not
the annexation of Belgium in some form or other was desirable.
Specifically, Herr Privy Councilor von Siemens spoke against the
acquisition of Belgian territory on the grounds that the bringing
of foreign populations within one's territorial borders should be
avoided. Furthermore, other committee members argued that the
annexation of Belgium would produce a very undesirable competition for German industry on the part of Belgian industry.
The majority of the gentlemen participating in the discussion,
however, argued against these remarks. Herr Privy Councilor
Hugenberg took the position that the German sphere of power
had to be very substantially expanded. The consequences of the
war will in themselves be unfavorable for the employers and
industry in many ways. There can be no doubt that the capacity
and willingness of the workers returning from the front to produce will suffer considerably when they are subordinated to fac-
tory discipline. One will probably have to count on a very
increased sense of power on the part of the workers and labor
unions, which will also find expression in increased demands on
the employers and for legislation. It would therefore be well advised, in order to avoid domestic difficulties, to distract the
attention of the people and to give phantasies concerning the
extension of German territory room to play.
Herr Privy Councilor Vogel of Chemnitz argued very decisively and passionately against the idea that any sort of fear

of Belgian competition could be decisive when it comes to carrying through a desired expansion of Germany. . . .

Herr Dr. Beumer of the Association of Industrialists in Rhineland and Westphalia underscored Herr Privy Councilor Hugenberg's concerns about the attitude of the workers. . . .

Dr. Stresemann pointed out to Herr Privy Councilor Hugenberg that the workers' chances of pushing through their demands always depend upon the economic structure of a country. If Germany were to experience a great economic upswing, then the workers and their organizations naturally would demand some benefit from it, irregardless of whether or not the war had taken place. The workers were in a position to push through such demands even before the war. On the other side, if there is an economic downswing, then the workers could not push through their demands no matter how powerful they felt. In general, it would be best to await the political development after the war. No one can say today which direction the trade union movement will take after the war. . . .

THE BETHMANN HOLLWEG
PROBLEM

Prior to the documentary discoveries of Fritz Fischer, Beth-
mann Hollweg was viewed by historians as a moderate, philo-
sophically inclined, and rather indecisive statesman. It was
presumed that Bethmann would have taken some enemy terri-
tory if Germany had won the war, but it was always noted that
Bethmann had refused or resisted committing himself to fixed
war aims. The September Memorandum (Document 26) discov-
ered by Fritz Fischer dealt a severe blow to this traditional por-
trait of the Chancellor. It appears that, before the German
setback on the Marne at least, Bethmann Hollweg was willing
to set down war aims for presentation at a projected peace con-
ference which could be termed moderate only in comparison to
those desired by the most extreme Pan-Germans. It must be kept
in mind that the memorandum was written in anticipation of a
rapid victory over France. It is most specific with regard to the
West, and least specific with regard to the East, where victory
remained to be won. As shall be shown in the section of inter-
pretations, the meaning of this memorandum has been hotly dis-
puted. Did Bethmann really hope to gain all its points? Was it
not, perhaps, an inescapable response to the broad public de-
mand for total victory in the heady atmosphere of the pre-Marne
period? Also, might it not have been written out of anxiety over
a protracted war with England and the need to control the con-
tinent in order to fight against the blockade imposed by the
mighty British navy? These, and other questions and interpreta-
tions have been raised by historians.

Whatever the case, the September Memorandum has cast a
shadow over Bethmann's wartime career. Was he ever a mod-
erate? Did he ever give up the 1914 war aims? Critics have argued

that Bethmann only slightly modified these aims after the Battle of the Marne at such times as he thought he might get a separate peace in the West or the East. Basically, however, the Chancellor's critics argue that he retained his aims out of conviction as well as out of the need to pacify right wing pressures. Bethmann's defenders insist that Bethmann was a moderate at heart and that his primary problem was right wing pressure to maintain excessive war aims. The report of Baron von Lerchenfeld, an astute observer on excellent terms with the Chancellor, seems to lend weight to the latter position. (Document 27) Throughout 1915–1916 Bethmann had struggled to have General von Falkenhayn removed as Chief of the General Staff and replaced by Hindenburg and Ludendorff. He disagreed with Falkenhayn's strategy and viewed Falkenhayn, with justification, as a political rival. Lerchenfeld's report, however, indicates that it was a desperate effort to bring the right wing annexationists to accept moderation. The problem remains, of course, what did Bethmann Hollweg consider to be moderate peace terms? In any case, as has been demonstrated, the new Supreme Command was anything but moderate. Perhaps the most concrete evidence of the actual content of Bethmann's war aims is provided by a letter Bethmann wrote to Chancellor Hertling a half year after the former's dismissal from office (Document 28). Bethmann wrote this letter to counter claims by Ludendorff that Bethmann had agreed to far-reaching aims at Kreuznach in April 1917. Ludendorff was hoping to use this to induce the government to promote the Supreme Command's aims at the forthcoming negotiations with the Russians at Brest-Litovsk.

26 FROM *Bethmann's Memorandum of September 9, 1914: "Provisional Notes on the Direction of Our Policy on the Conclusion of Peace"*

The "general aim of the war" was, for him, "security for the German Reich in west and east for all imaginable time. For this purpose France must be so weakened as to make her revival as a great power impossible for all time. Russia must be thrust back as far as possible from Germany's eastern frontier and her domination over the non-Russian vassal peoples broken."

1. *France.* The military to decide whether we should demand cession of Belfort and western slopes of the Vosges, razing of fortresses and cession of coastal strip from Dunkirk to Boulogne.

The ore-field of Briey, which is necessary for the supply of ore for our industry, to be ceded in any case.

Further, a war indemnity, to be paid in instalments; it must be high enough to prevent France from spending any considerable sums on armaments in the next 15-20 years.

Furthermore: a commercial treaty which makes France economically dependent on Germany, secures the French market for our exports and makes it possible to exclude British commerce from France. This treaty must secure for us financial and industrial freedom of movement in France in such fashion that German enterprises can no longer receive different treatment from French.

2. *Belgium.* Liége and Verviers to be attached to Prussia, a frontier strip of the province of Luxemburg to Luxemburg.

Question whether Antwerp, with a corridor to Liége, should also be annexed remains open.

At any rate Belgium, even if allowed to continue to exist as a state, must be reduced to a vassal state, must allow us to occupy

SOURCE (26). Reprinted from *Germany's Aims in the First World War* by Fritz Fischer. By permission of W.W. Norton & Company, Inc. Copyright 1961 by Droste Verlag und Druckerei GmbH, Dusseldorf. Translation Copyright © 1967 by W.W. Norton and Company, Inc., and Chatto & Windus, Ltd., pp. 103–105.

any militarily important ports, must place her coast at our disposal in military respects, must become economically a German province. Given such a solution, which offers the advantages of annexation without its inescapable domestic political disadvantages, French Flanders with Dunkirk, Calais and Boulogne, where most of the population is Flemish, can without danger be attached to this unaltered Belgium. The competent quarters will have to judge the military value of this position against England.

3. *Luxemburg.* Will become a German federal state and will receive a strip of the present Belgian province of Luxemburg and perhaps the corner of Longwy.

4. We must create a *central European economic association* through common customs treaties, to include France, Belgium, Holland, Denmark, Austria-Hungary, Poland [sic], and perhaps Italy, Sweden and Norway. This association will not have any common constitutional supreme authority and all its members will be formally equal, but in practice will be under German leadership and must stabilise Germany's economic dominance over Mitteleuropa.

5. *The question of colonial acquisitions,* where the first aim is the creation of a continuous Central African colonial empire, will be considered later, as will that of the aims to be realised *vis-à-vis* Russia.

6. A short provisional formula suitable for a possible preliminary peace to be found for a basis for the economic agreements to be concluded with France and Belgium.

7. *Holland.* It will have to be considered by what means and methods Holland can be brought into closer relationship with the German Empire.

In view of the Dutch character, this closer relationship must leave them free of any feeling of compulsion, must alter nothing in the Dutch way of life, and must also subject them to no new military obligations. Holland, then, must be left independent in externals, but be made internally dependent on us. Possibly one might consider an offensive and defensive alliance, to cover the colonies; in any case a close customs association, perhaps the cession of Antwerp to Holland in return for the right to keep a German garrison in the fortress of Antwerp and at the mouth of the Scheldt.

27 FROM   *Baron von Lerchenfeld,*
Bavarian Ambassador to Berlin, to Count von Hertling,
Minister-President of Bavaria, October 24, 1915

When I consider the mood of certain circles in Germany who daily increase their war aims, then I cannot be surprised at the attitude of our enemies. This war is the stupidity of the epoch. Germany, who entered the war to defend her skin, excepted, all the other nations began it without having any reasonable goal in mind. It is an unpolitical war based on national hatred, envy and ill-will, and for these reasons it is so difficult to see an end to it.

As Your Excellency knows, our fire-eaters are to be found in heavy industry in the West, which would like to eliminate Belgian competition, then in the scholarly world and among the Pan-Germans. Fortunately, this circle is narrowing. The number of those who are speaking of an acceptable peace even without great conquests is increasing, namely the number of those who do not consider the acquisition of Belgium as the *sine qua non* for the conclusion of peace. The view is gaining ground that the annexation of seven million embittered opponents of the Reich would hardly constitute a gain.

As Your Excellency knows, war aims have never been so extensive in the governing circles. Had it not been for the public mood which demanded so much and which could not be overlooked, the Chancellor would even last winter have prevented the outside world from taking the view that Germany wanted to conquer and keep all of Belgium, the northern coast of France, all of Poland and the Baltic provinces. Your Excellency will remember our discussions over these questions, when we always came to the conclusion that in view of the mood in the army and among the German people, it was completely impossible to conclude a peace which would involve giving up Belgium and other conquered territories and that therefore we would have to fight on.

In the meantime, this feeling has changed in the army as well

SOURCE (27). Translated by the editor from Bayerisches Geheimes Staatsarchiv, Abt. II, Nr. 912,21.

as in large sections of the public. The army will certainly hold out if it must. But the desire for an end to the fearful strains is evident among the officers and the men. And real war weariness is now being felt by the working and middle classes, who are feeling the effects of the war on their daily lives more and more. If a peace were to be concluded today which did not satisfy all aspirations, many would be disappointed, but in general it would still be welcomed.

The views of the Emperor and the Chancellor on the question of peace are known to Your Excellency. They want to take what the military situation will permit, but they do not want to carry on the war to eternity if the possibility should be offered of concluding peace on a more modest basis. Even the military does not think differently. In the latter circles one believes that with the defeat of Serbia, the opening up of the Danube to Constantinople and the driving of the English and the French from Gallipoli, the militarily attainable has reached its high point. Egypt remains still as a goal, but the prospects of carrying on the war there with success seem doubtful to many.

I believe that the key people will seize every opportunity to achieve peace once the Balkan undertaking is brought to a successful conclusion and that they are ready to make some sacrifice for this. Naturally only a sacrifice with some delayed profit (*lucrum cessans*), thus surrender of a larger or a smaller portion of the conquered territories.

That such a peace will meet with the strongest resistance from certain circles is sure, and it must therefore be covered by the authority of the most popular man in the German Empire. That is today Field Marshal von Hindenburg. The latter must conduct the peace negotiations alongside the Chancellor. The people will believe him when he says: This and no more was to be achieved.

28   FROM   *Bethmann Hollweg to
Count von Hertling, January 26, 1918*

With Your Excellency's permission, I wish to express myself in a completely confidential manner about a matter which, judging from the press, is beginning to occupy public attention in a very marked way.

In an article in yesterday's *Tag* there is the following passage:

"In the discussions concerning war aims which have taken place during the war between the Supreme Command and the Reich Chancellors, the leading military authorities have been informed repeatedly of the general program of the government. Naturally, the military plans of the Supreme Command have had to be arranged according to it. For example, one can achieve a complete peace of renunciation with a substantially smaller military effort and with incomparably less shedding of blood than is necessary for a peace guaranteeing Germany's future security."

I would like to agree with today's *Vorwärts* (the leading Socialist newspaper) which argues that this passage betrays in its tone and content the influence of the military. Despite these origins the statement is inaccurate and leads to false conclusions insofar as my tenure of office is concerned.

I have never given either the present or the previous Supreme Command a general war aims program with the direction that the war must be continued until it is attained. I have on the contrary insisted upon the necessity of utilizing every possible opportunity for the initiation of peace negotiations with the purpose of attaining for Germany what is recognized as valuable and possible in view of the military and political situation. I have never gone into precise detail (about war aims) but have limited myself to the following outlines: restoration of our colonies; in the West: preventing Belgium from becoming a hostile invasion gate; acquisition of Briey-Longwy if attainable, possibly by way of mutual frontier corrections; in the East: creation of the Polish Kingdom and improvement of the Prussian strategic

SOURCE (28). Translated by the editor from Microfilm of the Files of the German Foreign Office, U.C. Berkeley, File 1499, Frames D628338–D628343.

frontier while keeping the acquisition of new Polish population down to an irreducible minimum; possibly the creation of border states in Lithuania and Courland. I have always opposed the annexation of any considerable Polish territories.

My general policy concerning the desirability for the earliest possible opening of peace negotiations found official expression in our peace offer of December 12, 1916.

After the refusal of this offer and the opening of unrestricted submarine warfare, it was the Supreme Command which continually pressed for a setting down of a specific war aims program. They had never intimated with the single word that they needed this specification of war aims in order to determine their military measures. They could not even do this according to their general judgment concerning the military situation. They had opted for unrestricted submarine warfare because they could not end the war by military blows on the land. . . . *In actuality our military operations on land through the whole of last year until my departure remained exclusively defensive.*

Because His Majesty raised the wish of the Supreme Command for a fixing of a war aims program into a command, I finally gave way although I could not accept its having any practical significance. Thus there were the two days of negotiation at Kreuznach at the end of April 1917 at the conclusion of which the protocol of April 23 was drawn up. The conditions of peace stated in it were not formulated by me as my war aims program but rather by the Supreme Command as a *military necessity,* and it was much more extensive in the West as well as the East at the beginning of the negotiations than it was at the end. At that time there was no possibility of opening peace negotiations in which these war aims would form the basis of discussion. In agreement with State Secretary Zimmermann, who participated in these negotiations, I took the position that if the entire situation made it possible to implement this program at the time when peace negotiations could be opened, then I considered it acceptable in the interests of the German Reich. Therefore, this program was neither the basis for decisions over the further conduct of military operations nor the basis for a possible renewed peace offer from us, which was in any case ruled out by the entire political situation at that time.

The situation was changed when it became necessary to take a position on the Russian peace platform of "without annexations or indemnities." My intention of accepting this Russian formula expressly and simply foundered on the opposition of the Supreme Command which was supported by His Majesty. However, I declared in the Reichstag that I was willing to conclude a peace of understanding with Russia which would secure a neighborly relationship, while I refused to proclaim any war aims to the Western Powers. . . . In any case, by this a new situation was created vis à vis Russia which was entirely independent of the protocol of April 23. It was confirmed, broadened and extended to all of our enemies with the express agreement of the Supreme Command to the declared agreement of Reich Chancellor Michaelis to the Reichstag Resolution of July 19, in which even the clause "as I understand it" could not change anything. I cannot concede, therefore, that German policy in the presently impending peace negotiations or those about to be begun is in any way bound by agreements or measures taken by me—excluding of course the Polish Manifesto. The Kreuznach Protocol of April 23 is nothing but a private matter between the military and political leadership, which would not have bound even me if it had come to peace negotiations, much less does it have binding force for my successors. In actuality Your Excellency has established a completely independent program in repeated speeches and has given instructions for the negotiations at Brest-Litovsk on this basis alone. Insofar as the policy of my term of office is concerned, let me again state what I have already had the honor to tell Your Excellency orally. I have repeatedly emphasized in my talks with His Majesty that, in view of the fact that it has been shown since the beginning of the war that a complete defeat of our enemies is out of the question, a successful defense leading to the preservation of Germany's territorial integrity would mean her victory in the war. I persistently asked His Majesty—and I made a special point of this in my farewell audience—not to permit the conclusion of a peace on such a basis to be ruined by alleged military necessities since no one could judge as to whether what seems to be a military necessity today would be a military necessity after a generation. His Majesty agreed with this out of inner conviction every time and especially on July 16 he let me go saying that I could be completely unconcerned since his views on the conclusion of peace were exactly like mine. . . .

GERMANIZATION AND POPULATION TRANSFERS IN POLAND

29   FROM   *Memorandum of the*
Supreme Command on the Polish Border Strip,
July 5, 1918

Ethnic conflicts between Germans and Poles in the eastern
provinces of Prussia existed well before the war, and the govern-
ments of Bismarck (1871–1890) and Bülow (1900–1909), had
undertaken efforts to Germanize the Poles, expel Poles originally
resident in Russian Poland, increase German land ownership,
and encourage Germans to settle in the eastern areas. The pros-
pect of acquiring new Polish and eastern Jewish population
through annexations was not appealing to the wartime German
governments, but there was virtual consensus on the need to
acquire a frontier strip between the new Polish state Germany
planned to set up out of the areas formerly belonging to Russia.
From a strategic standpoint, the need for a stronger frontier
against Russia seemed absolutely necessary since the Russians
had taken advantage of the weak German frontier in the East
to ravage East Prussia in 1914. Politically, such a buffer seemed
desirable to keep Polish nationalist ideas and movements out
of the areas of Prussia containing substantial Polish populations.
To be effective, however, it was felt that such a buffer would
have to be German in fact as well as in name. The idea of ex-

SOURCE (29). Translated by the editor from Immanuel Geiss, *Der Polnische Grenzstreifen 1914–1918. Ein Beitrag zur deutschen Kriegszielpolitik im Ersten Weltkrieg* (Lübeck and Hamburg, Matthiesen Verlag, 1960) (Historische Studien, Heft 378), pp. 171–178.

*pelling the Poles and Jews in the proposed frontier strip was
discussed in high government circles as early as 1915 and, as the
documents below, which were discovered by Professor Fischer's
student, Dr. Immanuel Geiss, show, continued to be discussed
later in the war. It is difficult not to make an analogy with later
Nazi "resettlement" policies in the East, and the German arguments and plans seem particularly ironical in the light of contemporary Poland's post-1945 decision to drive out the Germans
living east of today's boundary between Germany and Poland,
the Oder-Neisse Line. It must be borne in mind, however, that
enslavement and extermination of Jews and Poles were never
contemplated by German leaders in the First World War.*

The extent of the danger which hovered over the entire German East is still little realized. If the Russians had taken advantage of the weakness of our border to carry out their attack of
October 1914 to both sides of the Vistula right away, then a
breakthrough into West Prussia and Posen and the cutting off
of East Prussia would have been unavoidable. One has to keep
in mind the unspeakable devastation of the battlefields of
northern France in order to comprehend the full implications
of what was then possible.

The danger of a repetition of such a situation remains because
of Germany's unfavorable military-geographical situation. One
cannot assume that our enemies will repeat the mistakes of 1914.
We must therefore give attention to the satisfactory securing of
our borders.

Alliances offer no certain protection. That is demonstrated by
the examples of Italy and Rumania. It is doubtful that Austria-
Hungary, in view of her domestic political development, will be
on our side in a future war. Poland will remain hostile so long
as the great-Polish dream remains unfulfilled.

An agreement with Poland according to which Polish units
and military exercises would be forbidden within a certain distance from the border is just as unsatisfactory as the right of
German occupation of militarily important Polish cities. No
state accepts such limits on its sovereignty over the long run.

Security that can be counted upon for the future and the guarantee of peace lie only in our own German strength. The creation of a wall of protection by moving forward the border of the Reich is an unavoidable necessity. . . .

The border strip will form the base of operations on the Prussian eastern border in a future war. The experiences on the West German border have shown the danger of a population hostile to Germany. It is now resulting in the creation of acceptable border conditions there through the liquidation of French property holdings and the settlement of Germans in the area. The Polish population presents the same kind of danger to our operations in the East. Here, too, we must create a reliable population by German colonization of the border strip and thus a wall between the future Kingdom of Poland and the Poles in Prussia.

The demand of the Supreme Command is completely in keeping with what authoritative government agencies and the best experts on our East have desired for national reasons.

Already on July 13, 1915, even before the taking of Warsaw, there was a discussion in the Reich Chancellery regarding a border strip to be separated from Poland. Then instructions were sent to the administrative chief in Poland to systematically but unobtrusively settle German refugees from Russia and also from the parts of Poland occupied by us in the border strip even during the war. The Germans already in the border strip area were to be kept there. . . .

At that time, therefore, the western portion of the border strip was prepared . . . by the Reich Government and, in fact, for an area greater than that which is demanded today for military reasons by the Supreme Command. The representative of the Prussian Finance Ministry supported the idea decisively on January 22, 1918. He reported that the Finance Minister would do everything he could to make the carrying out of the idea financially possible.

On the same occasion the President of the Royal Colonization Commission stated:

"I am of the view, and along with me practically all those who know our East, that a Polish State will be tolerable only if the geographical connection between our border provinces and the Kingdom of Poland is interrupted by a German colonized foreland. Therefore, for the security of Prussia and the German Empire it is necessary to have:

1. The shifting of the border to a line that can be held militarily.
2. The Germanization of the foreland gained by this shifting of the border."

That authoritative circles in the East agree with this view is demonstrated by the attached list of petitions which have been sent here by numerous organizations representing the eastern provinces, the cities, commerce, agriculture and colonization.[1]

Similarly, we have received declarations made publicly and privately by outstanding experts on our East.

The preliminary work of the experts and the discussions in Berlin have made plain that the difficulties involved in Germanizing the border strip have often been overestimated. The matter is not one of a complete emptying of the border strip, but rather primarily one of dominating the border area economically and politically. For this the transfer of Polish landed property, and to be sure only the large and a part of the middle-sized Polish landed holdings, to German hands would suffice. The President of the Royal Colonization Commission and former District President v. Schwerin, one of the best experts on contemporary colonization practice, completely agrees with this view.

According to the unanimous view of the experts, there can be no question about the ability to carry out such a colonization technically. The words of the President of the Royal Colonization Commission, with which the other experts agree completely, are repeated here:

"If it is asked if such a measure can be carried out, then I answer: 'It is only a question of will!' It depends alone upon whether one's will is stronger or less strong. New colonization with German peasants will create no difficulty at all. We can expect plenty of colonists, so that we would also not be lacking in people if the border strip would be made, as I hope, very large."

[1] Twenty-five such petitions were appended to this memorandum. It is significant, of course, that these petitions were sent to the Supreme Command directly rather than, as might be expected, to the political leaders in Berlin.— G.D.F.

Reports from German colonists in Russia and the investigations made of German colonies in Poland support this view. In the years after the war we can expect a stream of German returnees, and, because of the financing necessary for this re-settlement, it lies completely in the hands of the state authorities to direct this stream in a manner demanded by the interests of the Reich. . . .

PART TWO

Post-1945 Documents and Interpretations
B. The Interpretations

30 FROM   *Hans W. Gatzke*
Germany's Drive to the West

The first major post–World War Two study of Germany's war aims in the First World War was the work of an American, Hans W. Gatzke, now Professor of History at Yale University. Although Gatzke had access to the captured German war documents, the chief contribution of Germany's Drive to the West *lay in its emphasis on the role of interest groups in the promotion of German war aims and on the relationship between domestic politics and annexationism. Gatzke analyzed the public support for annexationism, the so-called war aims movement (Kriegszielbewegung) as well as the majority support for annexationism (Kriegszielmehrheit) in the Reichstag before the passage of the peace resolution. While noting strong annexationist tendencies within the civilian government of Germany, Gatzke maintained the traditional view of Bethmann Hollweg as a moderate and continued to differentiate between the civilian and the military authorities. Gatzke did suggest an element of continuity in German imperialism, however, by noting that Germany's efforts to control France's iron ore mines before the war culminated in the demands for the annexation of Briey-Longwy during the war.*

SOURCE (30). Reprinted with permission of the publishers from Hans W. Gatzke, *Germany's Drive to the West (Drang nach Westen)*. *A Study of Germany's Western War Aims During the First World War*, Baltimore, Maryland, The Johns Hopkins Press, 1950, pp. 38–47, 288–294.

THE KRIEGSZIELBEWEGUNG

The close community of interests and personnel between the Pan-German League and German heavy industry necessarily suggested concerted action. An alliance between the financial resources of the latter and the effective propaganda machine of the former naturally presented obvious advantages to both. The first to think of such an alliance was Heinrich Class, who brought it to the attention of Alfred Hugenberg, representative of heavy industry, as early as August 1914. Hugenberg, Class tells us, shared his views: "So we went to work immediately; the German *Kriegszielbewegung,* which played an important role in the course of the great conflict, had begun." A plan of campaign was drawn up in subsequent discussions between Class and Hugenberg.

Hugenberg, whom we have already encountered, had himself been one of the founders of the Pan-German League. In 1909 he had become Chief Director of Krupp's, a position which made him particularly suitable as a link between the two leading annexationist factions. His talent for organization, moreover, made him a valuable asset not only to the Krupps, but to German heavy industry in general. In some ways he might be considered its most influential and most typical figure. Reserved, immobile, stubborn, and ruthless, he quickly gained the confidence of all the great in Germany's iron, steel, and coal industry. "Hugenberg is not a man, he is a wall," secretive and strong like "the vault of a great bank."

Shortly after he began his work with Krupp, Hugenberg was made joint chairman of the Chambers of Commerce of Essen, Mühlheim, and Oberhausen. In 1912 he became President of the *Bergbaulicher Verein,* which represented the interests of all large Ruhr concerns. Hugenberg, in co-operation with Emil Kirdorf, used this position to build up a most important organization, the so-called *Wirtschaftsvereinigung.* Its purpose was to concentrate in one hand the various financial contributions which the Ruhr industrialists were constantly called upon to make to charitable and political organizations. A committee under the direction of Hugenberg decided in each case whether a cause warranted the financial backing of heavy industry. Many political and other groups, by accepting such backing, put themselves under the control of the Hugenberg committee. Hugenberg had thus become the holder of the Ruhr industry's purse strings, a position which he held until long after the war.

As the opening move of the *Kriegszielbewegung* Class instigated a meeting, in late September of 1914, of various industrial, commercial, and agricultural organizations, to express the unanimous confidence of Germany's economy in the successful completion of the war. The list of speakers was impressive (Dr. Kaempf, Progressive and President of the Reichstag, Count von Schwerin-Löwitz, President of the Prussian Lower House, Roetger, head of the *Bund der Industriellen,* and Wolfgang Kapp, famous annexationist) and the general tenor of the speeches delivered was annexationist, though in rather veiled terms. In a telegram addressed to the Emperor, the participants expressed hope for a peace "which will correspond to the enormous sacrifices of this war and make its repetition impossible."

In October 1914, the *Zentralverband Deutscher Industrieller,* the *Bund der Landwirte,* and the Conservative Party met, on invitation from Hugenberg, to discuss the problem of food supply. In November the Pan-German League joined in, and the discussion shifted from grain to war aims. As its first action this newly-constituted group asked Class and Hugenberg to prepare a program of war aims based on the Class memorandum of September 1914. This program was presented at a meeting of these organizations on December 15, 1914. The mention of Stinnes indicates that probably other industrialists besides Hugenberg were present. On this occasion the Conservatives, led by Westarp, opposed some of the more far-reaching among the Class-Hugenberg proposals, and when they found no sympathy among the other delegates present, they withdrew at a later meeting their active participation in the *Kriegszielbewegung.* This did not mean that the Conservative Party was opposed to annexations, but merely that its leaders objected to some of the exaggerated aims of the Pan-Germans and their friends, considering them unrealistic and utopian. Several Conservatives moreover, such as Roesicke and von Wangenheim, did not share their party's views and continued to take part in future meetings.

In the meantime, as we have seen already, Class had sent out the 1,950 copies of his own memorandum. Among the many enthusiastic replies was a letter from Hugenberg, expressing the agreement of himself and of "the other industrial gentlemen." In late January 1915, the annexationists got together again, to continue their discussion of the memorandum which Class and Hugenberg had worked out during the preceding months. Their plan was to use this memorandum as a declaration of the leading industrial and agricultural organizations, and, if possible, of the parties of the *Kriegszielmehrheit* as well. The January meeting was attended by some thirty persons, Hugenberg presiding. Of leading industrialists, Kirdorf, Stinnes, Beukenberg, Reusch, and von Borsig were present. The *Bund der Industriellen,* in which Stresemann played a leading role, was represented by its chairman Friedrichs, and the *Bund der Landwirte* by Baron von Wangenheim and Roesicke. Besides Class, the Pan-Germans had sent General von Gebsattel, Admiral von Grumme-Douglas, and Johannes Neumann, a Lübeck senator.

Class delivered the main address, based on his own memorandum. It was received in deep silence and without comment, until Hugo Stinnes rose to speak. Here is Class' description:

"Stinnes was no speaker. His sentences kept flowing evenly, without a raising or lowering of his voice. . . . But there could be no doubt—in spite of his cold and businesslike manner, he was quite aware of the importance of our age. One can imagine, therefore, the impression it made when he put the whole weight of his personality behind my proposals . . . promising to use his influence with the *Zentralverband Deutscher Industrieller* to urge their acceptance by that group."

Hugo Stinnes, whose speech made such an impression, was the youngest at the meeting. Barely 44 years old, he already was one of the wealthiest and most influential of European industrialists. In addition to his chief enterprise, the *Deutsch-Luxemburgische Bergwerks—und Hütten A. G.,* covering large regions in the Ruhr and in Alsace-Lorraine, he controlled—together with Thyssen— the *Rheinisch-Westphälische Elektrizitätswerks A. G.,* which supplied most of western Germany with electricity. During and after the war he expanded his holding to include not only additional mines and iron-works, but also shipping companies, power plants, paper works, hotels, and newspapers, building up one of the world's largest vertical trusts. Albert Ballin once said: "As some children cannot let alone a piece of cake, or some men a beautiful woman, so Stinnes cannot let business alone; he wants to make everything his own, even if it should happen to belong to somebody else."

Like most of his colleagues among Germany's captains of industry, Stinnes preferred the actuality of power to its outward manifestations. He never abandoned the simplicity of dress and manner which made him like one of his workers, "a walking piece of coal." His business transactions were usually carried on in an atmosphere of secrecy, which only helped to magnify their importance in the eyes of outsiders. Already during his lifetime, and still more so after his early death in 1924, the figure of Stinnes, unlike that of any of his colleagues, became almost legendary. His pale face, his black, pointed beard, and his manner of speaking coolly and dispassionately in a "weary whisper," earned him names like "Assyrian King," "Flying Dutchman," or "Christ of Coal." His influence on the political affairs of Germany is difficult to determine, since most of his political, like his economic activities, were carefully hidden from public scrutiny. That his influence was considerable can be gathered from numerous references in contemporary accounts. Especially during the second half of the war, when much of the Government's actual power was centered in the Supreme Command, Stinnes paid frequent visits to headquarters and seems to have been consulted on many questions. His friendship with General Ludendorff was particularly close.

To return to the annexationist meeting in Berlin—once Stinnes had endorsed the views of Heinrich Class, they found immediate and full support of those present. Baron von Wangenheim, welcoming the possibility of large-scale German settlements, notably in the east, pledged the support of the Agrarian League. Friedrichs added his approval in the name of German industry. After general agreement had thus been registered, a detailed discussion of each point of the Hugenberg-Class memorandum followed, in which everybody took part. At the close of the meeting, its oldest participant, Emil Kirdorf, urged the dissemination of the war aims agreed on at the meeting among the whole German people, regardless of governmental opposition.

Kirdorf was another outstanding member of the aristocracy of coal and iron, in a class with Thyssen and Stinnes. Founder of the *Gelsenkirchener Bergwerks A. G.* (the largest Ruhr enterprise, employing 65,000 workers) he was the only great industrialist who openly and consistently supported the annexationists. A small and unpretentious man, much like his chief rival, August Thyssen, this "Bismarck of German coal mining" concealed, behind a genial front, an iron will and ruthless determination, which appeared in his many conflicts with Thyssen and in his stubborn fight against labor unions.

Class and Hugenberg, with the help of the latter's associate, Hirsch, now incorporated the results of the January meeting into a second draft of their memorandum. In a later session, this version was adopted and signed by the representatives of the various economic organizations which had participated in the preliminary discussions—the *Zentralverband Deutscher Industrieller,* the *Bund der Industriellen,* the *Bund der Landwirte,* the *Deutscher Bauernbund,* and the *Reichsdeutscher Mittelstandsverband.* On March 10, 1915, this declaration of the five economic organizations was presented to the German Chancellor. Simultaneously, the same organizations, with added support from the commercial *Hansa Bund,* petitioned the Reichstag to permit the public discussion of peace aims, expressing the hope "that our German Fatherland shall emerge from its fight for existence—which has been forced upon it—greater and stronger, with secured frontiers in the west and the east and with the European and colonial extensions of territory necessary for the maintenance of our sea power as well as for military and economic reasons."

It should be noted that for tactical reasons the chief annexationist wire-pullers, the Pan-Germans and industrialists, do not appear in either petition, except indirectly. To remedy this omission, Hugenberg, Stinnes, and Kirdorf, together with several historians and geographers and with the Westphalian branches of the National Liberal and Center Parties, issued an additional memorandum in favor of annexations in March of 1915. As a further consolidation of the annexationist front, the collaborator of Class and Hugenberg, Dr. Hirsch, also tried to establish an alliance between the signatories of the Hugenberg-Class memorandum and the bourgeois and annexationist parties of the Reichstag. At a meeting on May 1, however, both the Conservatives and the Center expressed their preference for independent action. The result of this decision, the conversation between Bethmann and the representatives of the annexationist parties on May 13, 1915, we have already discussed.

But even if this attempt to link the *Kriegszielbewegung* and the *Kriegszielmehrheit* failed, the annexationist parties, especially the National Liberals and the Free Conservatives, were very much in favor of the aims proclaimed by the Pan-Germans and the Economic Organizations. Even the Conservatives, in spite of their earlier secession, still maintained "close contact and agreement" with the *Kriegszielbewegung*. Roesicke and Admiral von Grumme-Douglas, besides holding leading positions in the Agrarian and Pan-German Leagues respectively, also played prominent roles in the Conservative Party. Further co-operation between the various annexationist groups was maintained through the *Auskunftsstelle Vereinigter Verbände,* founded by Dr. Poensgen, which counted among its members Professor Dietrich Schäfer, Bassermann, Stresemann, and Matthias Erzberger. Its purpose was the collection and co-ordination of the various annexationist programs and pronouncements and their propagation through meetings and publications.

On May 20, 1915, the petition of March 10, in almost its original form, was again addressed to the Chancellor and the Ministries of the various federal states. Besides the original five organizations, a sixth, the *Christliche Deutsche Bauernvereine* added its signature, thus making it the well-known "Petition of the Six Economic Organizations." Although not quite so radical as the memorandum of Heinrich Class, it clearly shows the influence of its Pan-German and industrial godfathers. To satisfy commercial circles it demanded "a colonial empire adequate to satisfy Germany's manifold economic interests." Agrarian needs were to be met "by annexation of at least parts of the Baltic Provinces and of those territories which lie to the south of them. . . . The great addition to our manufacturing resources which we anticipate in the west, must be counterbalanced by an equivalent annexation of agricultural territory in the east."

It was in regard to the west that the petition was most emphatic and specific. The future which it painted for Belgium was much like the proposal Bethmann Hollweg had made to the representatives of the bourgeois parties on May 13, 1915. From France the Six Associations demanded the coastal districts, including the hinterland, as far as the mouth of the Somme, to improve Germany's strategic position against England. In addition they asked for the district of Briey, the coal country of the *Départements du*

Nord and *Pas-de-Calais,* and the fortresses of Verdun, Longwy, and Belfort. Class' suggestion for "land free from inhabitants" was not included in the petition, a fact for which the Conservatives claim credit.

The total area that the Six Organizations demanded from Western Europe amounted to some 50,000 square miles, with a population of *ca.* 11 million. The arguments used to justify these annexations ranged from the rather vague—"the prize of victory must correspond to our sacrifice"—to most specific military and economic considerations:

"The iron-ore and coal districts mentioned above are demanded by our military necessities and not by any means in the interests only of our manufacturing development. . . . As a raw material for the production of pig iron and steel . . . , minette is being employed more and more. . . . If the output of minette were interrupted, the war would be as good as lost."

This, however, might easily happen, since the mining and industrial region of Lorraine was directly in the shadow of French guns:

"Does anyone believe that the French, in the next war, would neglect to place long-range guns in Longwy and Verdun and would allow us to continue the extraction of ore and the production of pig-iron? . . . Hence the security of the German Empire in a future war imperatively demands the possession of the whole minette-bearing district of Luxemburg and Lorraine, together with the fortifications of Longwy and Verdun, without which this district cannot be held."

Most of these arguments were demolished almost immediately. It was maintained, for instance, that strategically the possession of the French coast would not in the least ensure Germany's domination of the English Channel, especially in the age of the airplane of which people were just becoming aware; and economically, Belgium and northern France, far from having an excess of coal, had to import that commodity to meet the needs of their considerable industries, and thus were an economic liability: Still, we must realize that there were considerable advantages to be gained for German industry from these western annexations, such as the domination, and, if necessary, elimination, of Belgian and

French industrial competition; or the assurance to Germany's iron masters of a continued supply of ore from eastern France. We have already treated the significance of this last question during the pre-war period and have traced the attempts of Germany's industrialists to solve it by economic penetration of French Lorraine and Normandy. The growing French demand for the elimination in the future of this German influence threatened German industry with the loss of these valuable sources of supply, even if the war ended on a *status quo ante* basis. For Germany's heavy industry, therefore, it was a question of all or nothing. Either Germany would gain complete control of France's iron supply, or else she would lose even the small foothold she had gained before the war. It is this fact which explains the deep interest of German industry in the war aims problem. . . .

* * *

CONCLUSION

We have come to the end of the Great War and Germany's attempts to extend her political and economic influence over much of the European continent and overseas. The anti-climax to more than four years of great expectations did not come until several months later, when the war aims of the Allies won their triumphal victory at the Peace Conference of Paris. Instead of acquiring the ore basin of Briey and Longwy, Germany had to cede Alsace and Lorraine to France. Instead of gaining all or part of Belgium, she was forced to give up the districts of Eupen and Malmédy. The dream of a large *Mittelafrika* not only failed to materialize, but Germany lost even the colonies she held before 1914. And finally, far from being able to regain the expenses of the war from their enemies, the Germans had to shoulder the whole burden of misery and destruction which the war had caused to all the world. Annexationism, as the final outcome of the war showed, was a universal problem, not confined to one particular nation. What differences existed between the two groups of powers were of objective rather than of principle. Viewed in the light of four years of annexationist propaganda and the treaties of Brest-Litovsk and Bucharest, the kind of peace settlement which a victorious Germany would have imposed upon her western op-

ponents would most likely have equalled, if not surpassed, the
one she was forced to sign at Versailles. Nevertheless, the German
people have been almost unanimous in their condemnation of
the Versailles Treaty; and ironically enough, the most vociferous
denunciations of its terms have come from the very circles that
were most outspoken in favor of annexations during the First
World War.

It is difficult to sum up a topic as complex as the present one,
not the least because it is a study of unfulfilled ambitions. As
with any development which fails to reach its logical conclusion,
a discussion of the effects of German expansionist plans on the
history of the Empire will move as much in the realm of speculation as in the realm of fact. Still, there are two final questions that
should be answered on the basis of the material presented in this
study. One concerns the general influence of the problem of war
aims on German affairs during the war; the second the role which
various factors and factions within Germany played in the propagation of war aims—in other words: who was responsible for the
Drang nach Westen?

In the field of foreign affairs, the question uppermost in the
minds of historians has been whether the continued declaration
of German war aims was responsible for the failure to reach a
peace of understanding during the course of the war. To answer
this question one has to consider not merely Germany's war aims,
but those of her opponents as well. To use a concrete example:
while the problem of Belgium, because of Great Britain's insistence on Belgian independence, developed into one of the crucial
obstacles to a negotiated peace, the problem of Alsace-Lorraine
was just as important to Germany as Belgium was to Great
Britain. If Germany failed to renounce Belgium, France made it
perfectly clear that she never intended to give up her demand
for the return of Alsace-Lorraine. Nevertheless, there were several
situations—and here we enter the realm of speculation—in which
a clear statement on Belgium might have resulted in peace negotiations. England might have been willing to break her commit-
ments under the secret treaties of London and make a separate
peace with Germany; or else she could bring sufficient pressure to
bear on France, so that the latter would give up her aims in
Alsace-Lorraine; or maybe a clear German statement would have
strengthened the peace-loving groups within the Allied nations,

who in turn might have forced their governments to negotiate peace with Germany. Considering these various possibilities, a clear German statement on Belgium would have been decidedly worth trying. Not to have made it remains a grave blunder of German foreign policy during the World War.

In trying to evaluate the influence of war aims upon domestic affairs in Germany, we are on somewhat safer ground. Entering the war with a number of internal problems, the solution of which had long been overdue, the German people soon found this solution postponed not only for the duration of the war, but most likely for an indefinite period. Annexationism in its most outspoken form became the main province of the upper classes, in their vain hope of maintaining their own political and social supremacy. To the lower classes it appeared, with much justification, that the war was being carried on for the sake of foreign gains, which in turn would only serve to perpetuate domestic injustices. To have thus maintained and intensified the political, social, and economic cleavages among the German people at one of the most critical periods of its existence is one of the serious responsibilities of annexationism.

How large a part these foreign and domestic influences of annexationism played in shaping the history of the German Empire during the World War is difficult to say. To realize their magnitude, we do well to remember the effect of war aims on the dismissal of such important political figures as Bethmann Hollweg and Kühlmann, both of them victims of the annexationists. We should also remember the many attempts to arrive at a negotiated peace settlement, all of them condemned to failure because of the war aims, declared or implied, of the two groups of belligerents. And finally, we should bear in mind the internal strife and disunity created by four years of wrangling over war aims which contributed decisively to the weakening and final collapse of Imperial Germany.

As to the problem of responsibility, it is a more difficult and controversial one. The great number of factors involved in the propagation of German war aims makes it difficult to assign to each a due share of liability for the blunders committed in the handling of the war aims problem. Although the German government entered the war without specific aims, it would have been unrealistic, after the successes of Germany's armed forces, to expect this state of affairs to last. Germany in 1914 was no longer the saturated power she had been under Bismarck. An extension of territory, the gain of new fields of commercial activity, and the acquisition of additional sources of raw material were looked upon as absolute necessities to a growing and highly industrialized country. The German government, therefore, should have drawn up a realistic program of war aims, moderate in scope but specific in character. This program should have been so designed as to concentrate on one of the major fields of possible expansion—east, west, or overseas—and thus, by driving a wedge between the Allied Powers, make possible the kind of negotiated peace which had become an unavoidable necessity since the failure of the Schlieffen plan in 1914. In addition to such specific aims, a series of general principles might have completed a program which, much in the way of President Wilson's Fourteen Points, would have won the support of the majority of Germans, thus making possible a more effective conduct of the war.

Instead, the Imperial government preferred to leave the question of war aims vague and undecided, clinging to the concept of a war of defense, which few people in Germany and still fewer outside really believed. Left without direction from above but encouraged by the ambiguity of official pronouncements, the German people embarked upon a heated controversy over war aims, which destroyed the last vestige of internal unity created by the outbreak of war. Instead of counteracting this confusion of minds by publishing a definite set of aims, the government preferred to suppress this public discussion, thus only increasing its intensity. Abroad, the failure to come out clearly for or against annexations, viewed in connection with these unofficial utterances in favor of far-reaching war aims, created an atmosphere of suspicion, which made any peace short of complete German or Allied victory impossible.

The responsibility for initiating this policy of vagueness and confusion belongs to Bethmann Hollweg. It was he who set the style for the kind of war aims statement open to almost any interpretation which was then followed by his two successors. While moderate in his aims the uncertainty of Bethmann's statements was a direct boon to his annexationist opponents, to whose attacks he finally succumbed. Bethmann's chief motive was a sincere desire to maintain Germany's internal unity by avoiding the disagreement inherent in the vital question of war aims. But even though his own aims were moderate it would be incorrect to consider the Chancellor averse to any expansion whatsoever. Like most of his countrymen, Bethmann was willing to await the outcome of war before deciding on a definite set of aims. Any premature declaration, he felt, would only limit this German choice. Where Bethmann differed from his successors was in his willingness to give up whatever hopes of gain he had, if in return a negotiated peace could be won. The question what might have happened if his dismissal had not come in the midst of the Papal peace move, is one of the most interesting points of speculation of the whole World War.

After the middle of 1917, the direction of affairs shifted from the hands of the political to those of Germany's military authorities. While outwardly the ambiguous policy on war aims continued, there was no longer much doubt as to the annexationist ambitions of those in command. The fact that this change occurred when popular sentiment in Germany and elsewhere grew increasingly desirous of peace, was most deplorable. The primary motive behind the war aims of the Supreme Command was the attempt to secure, once and for all, Germany's position in Western Europe. Ludendorff's views on the fundamental strategic significance of Belgium should have made him realize, however, that Germany's desire of keeping Belgium was matched by an equally strong Allied determination to prevent Germany from gaining too powerful a position there. As the war progressed, it became increasingly clear that there were only two possible alternatives: a German victory, enabling her to do with Belgium as she pleased, or a negotiated peace, requiring first and foremost that Germany give up Belgium. There appear to have been a few brief instances during the spring of 1918, especially in his conversations with von Haeften, when Ludendorff was more moderate on the subject of Belgium; though to declare this moderation openly, he felt, might seriously affect the morale of the German army. The view held by Bethmann Hollweg, that it was a sufficiently great achievement for Germany to have withstood successfully the large coalition of her enemies, was foreign to the military mind. Both Hindenburg and Ludendorff shared the mistaken belief that the average soldier would only continue fighting if he was shown sufficiently large war aims. If anything, the opposite was true. As the hardships of war increased most soldiers were indignant at the suggestion of continuously risking their lives for the sake of ultimate material gains.

Although politically unsound, the strategic motives behind the army's stubborn annexationism are understandable from the point of view of its own limited, military sphere. The unfortunate part was that the Supreme Command gained such a predominating influence over the direction of German affairs. The absence of any suitable counterweight in the political field tended to centralize complete political as well as military responsibility in the hands of General Ludendorff. His strong and domineering personality played a not insignificant part in this process. As a result the necessary and mutually corrective division of control between military and political authorities disappeared. In addition we must remember the close relationship between Ludendorff and the small but powerful annexationist minority, based on a community of war aims and a deep affinity of social background and political belief. The constant contact between the Supreme Command and Germany's barons of industry suggests that the motives which prompted the annexationism of the German army were not always and exclusively military. Ludendorff's uncompromising adherence to strong war aims was the most important single influence in Germany's misguided efforts to extend her sphere of influence to the west. Although his attitude was determined by the needs of his country, these needs were seen entirely through the eyes of his profession and class. On the one hand they included the necessary strategic improvements enabling the General Staff to be prepared for the next war; and on the other such material and territorial gains as would ensure the maintenance of the existing political and social order. There was really little difference between Ludendorff and most of the radical annexationists, except that the General was in a position where he could enforce his annexationist views.

In discussing the attitude of the German people towards war aims, we have distinguished between the large and inarticulate masses and their parliamentary representatives. The views of the first group are difficult to ascertain. It seems fairly certain, however, that the majority of Germans, under the influence of early military successes, were in favor of more or less strong aims. As the war progressed, this stand became more moderate. The change, which became pronounced some time in 1916, ended in a widespread longing for peace among the lower classes. This fact was not due to any greater degree of political insight on the part of this group over its social and economic betters, but rather to the fact that the common people in Germany suffered more deeply from the hardships of war. It was partly for that reason that the change of attitude from annexationism to moderation was not reflected in the German Reichstag until the middle of 1917. Despite the absence of constitutional provisions to that effect, the influence of the Reichstag became ever greater as the war continued. Its role in the dismissal of both Bethmann Hollweg and Michaelis signified the change from bureaucratic to parliamentary regime. But unfortunately little use was made of this newly-won power to demand a voice in the government's foreign policy. The 1917 Peace Resolution was as far as the majority of the Reichstag was willing to go. As soon as the military situation improved, it reverted to its earlier acquiescence in the decisions of Germany's political and military leaders, as shown in the stand taken on the Treaty of Brest-Litovsk. In the majority of its middle class, the German people resembled those "tree-frog annexationists" whose war aims changed with the news from the front. Only the Socialists, with some exceptions, maintained a consistently and courageously anti-annexationist platform from the first day of the war to the last.

There remains the small group of annexationists to which we have devoted so much of our discussion. Granted the German civil government was too vague and not always moderate in its aims, granted many Germans changed their views according to the success or failure of the armed forces, still there were several critical situations in which the feeling of moderation might have gained the upper hand had it not been for the vigilance of the annexationist groups and individuals organized behind the *Kriegszielbewegung*. It was this numerically unimportant but politically, financially, and intellectually powerful minority which took the lead in the evolution of a German program of war aims. Among these radical annexationists, the great industrialists played a particularly important role. There may be some doubt as to the motives of some of the members of the *Kriegszielbewegung* whose patriotism was more important than their greed; there is no doubt as we deal with men like Thyssen, Stinnes, Kirdorf, Hugenberg,

Kloeckner, Beukenberg, and their lesser known associates. To these men Germany's westward expansion meant specific material gains, and Germany's failure to expand meant specific material losses.

It was a combination of elements, then, industrialists, Pan-Germans, the parties of the Right, and the Supreme Command, that was responsible for the stubborn propagation of large war aims, which condemned the German people to remain at war until the bitter end. Each of these forces had its own particular reasons for wanting to hold out for far-reaching territorial gains; yet one aim most of them had in common—to ensure through a successful peace settlement the continuation of the existing order, to their own advantage, and to the political and economic detriment of the majority of the German people.

31 FROM   *Fritz Fischer*
        Germany's Aims in the First World War

As noted in the introduction to this volume, it was Professor Fritz Fischer of the University of Hamburg who made the war aims issue the subject of ferocious debate among historians. His sensational study, Griff nach der Weltmacht, *with its somewhat misleading title (literally: 'Grasp for World Power') was a massively documented attempt to demonstrate the continuity of German imperialism, the chief responsibility of Germany for the outbreak of the war in 1914, the similarity of the war aims of the civilian and military authorities, and the broad support which annexationism received from large segments of German society. Since 1961, a surprising consensus has developed among German and American historians concerning at least some of Fischer's*

SOURCE (31). Reprinted from *Germany's Aims in the First World War* by Fritz Fischer. By Permission of W.W. Norton & Company, Inc. Copyright 1961 by Droste Verlag und Druckerei GmbH, Dusseldorf. Translation Copyright © 1967 by W.W. Norton & Company, Inc. and Chatto & Windus, Ltd., pp. 87–89, 91–92, 105–106, 155–157, 313–316, 342–348, 350–351, 507–509, 607–608.

contentions. It seems clear that Bethmann Hollweg, the Kaiser, and the military authorities consciously risked a world war in 1914, although opinions differ as to whether this risk was taken out of an aggressive effort to secure Germany's status as a world power once and for all or as an act of despair designed to bolster Austria-Hungary and break the ring of enemies surrounding the Central Powers. Similarly, a more critical attitude is being taken toward Bethmann Hollweg and there is an increasing recognition of the continuity of German imperialism in the late nineteenth and early twentieth centuries.

A. THE WAR GUILT QUESTION

The basic contention of Fischer's long introductory section on this subject is that Bethmann Hollweg's fundamental concern in the July 1914 crisis was not to prevent war but rather to secure British neutrality and to put Russia in the wrong by having the latter power mobilize first. In this way, Germany would succeed in breaking the Triple Entente and in securing the support of the German Social Democrats in a defensive war against the Tzarist autocracy.

WHO WAS 'GUILTY'?

There is no question but that the conflict of military and political interests, of resentment and ideas, which found expression in the July crisis, left no government of any of the European powers quite free of some measure of responsibility—greater or smaller—for the outbreak of the war in one respect or another. It is, however, not the purpose of this work to enter into the familiar controversy, on which whole libraries have been written, over the question of war guilt, to discuss exhaustively the responsibility of the individual statesmen and soldiers of all the European powers concerned, or to pass final judgment on them. We are concerned solely with the German leaders' objectives and with the policy actually followed by them in the July crisis, and that only in so far as their policy throws light on the postulates and origins of Germany's war aims.

It must be repeated: given the tenseness of the world situation in 1914—a condition for which Germany's world policy, which had already led to three dangerous crises (those of 1905, 1908 and 1911), was in no small measure responsible—any limited or local war in Europe directly involving one great power must inevitably carry with it the imminent danger of a general war. As Germany willed and coveted the Austro-Serbian war and, in her confidence in her military superiority, deliberately faced the risk of a conflict with Russia and France, her leaders must bear a substantial share of the historical responsibility for the outbreak of general war in 1914. This responsibility is not diminished by the fact that at the last moment Germany tried to arrest the march of destiny, for her efforts to influence Vienna were due exclusively to the threat of British intervention and, even so, they were half-hearted, belated and immediately revoked.

It is true that German politicians and publicists, and with them the entire German propaganda machine during the war and German historiography after the war—particularly after Versailles—have invariably maintained that the war was forced on Germany, or at least (adopting Lloyd George's dictum, made for political reasons, that "we all stumbled into the war") that Germany's share of the responsibility was no greater that that of the other participants. But confidential exchanges between Germany and Austria, and between the responsible figures in Germany itself, untinged by any propagandist intent, throw a revealing spotlight on the real responsibility.

A few weeks after the outbreak of war, during the crises on the Marne and in Galicia, the Austrians asked urgently for German help against the superior Russian armies facing them. It was refused. Count Tisza then advised Berchtold to tell the Germans: "That we took our decision to go to war on the strength of the express statements both of the German Emperor and of the German Imperial Chancellor that they regarded the moment as suitable and would be glad if we showed ourselves in earnest."

Just three years later, on August 14, 1917, at the climax of a heated debate whether the war should be continued in the interest of Germany's war aims, Austria-Hungary's Foreign Minister, Count Czernin, told his German interlocutors excitedly: "It was not Austria alone that began the war then." Characteristically, the official German minutes in the Imperial Chancellery left Czernin's next sentence incomplete and passed over the retorts of the German statesmen, Michaelis, Kühlmann and Helfferich, but the minutes of the Army High Command (the OHL) gave the sentence in full: "Germany demanded that the ultimatum to Serbia should be drawn up in those sharp terms."

In February, 1918, again, Czernin asked Berchtold if he would object if he (Czernin) published a letter written by him to Tisza shortly before the outbreak of war, which showed: "what strong efforts Germany was making at that time to hold us to a hard line, and how our alliance might have been in danger if we had given way."

There is other evidence to confirm that the Central Powers in no way 'slid into war'. Josef Baernreither, an Austrian politician who was entirely well disposed towards the Reich and was a leading champion of the Mitteleuropa idea during the war, made the following entry on the July crisis in his diary for December, 1914:

"The Germans were afraid that we would refuse to go with them if the war broke out over some question remote from us. At Algeciras we were still 'seconds': later, not even that; in the Morocco crisis we did not stand by Germany firmly. But war was bound to come, as things had developed, through the faults of German and Austro-Hungarian diplomacy. So when the Sarajevo murder took place, Germany seized her opportunity and made an Austrian grievance her signal for action. That is the history of the war."

• • •

The official documents afford ample proofs that during the July crisis the Emperor, the German military leaders and the Foreign Ministry were pressing Austria-Hungary to strike against Serbia without delay, or alternatively agreed to the despatch of an ultimatum to Serbia couched in such sharp terms as to make war between the two countries more than probable, and that in doing so they deliberately took the risk of a continental war against Russia and France. But the decisive point is that, as we now know—although for a long time it was not admitted—these groups were not alone. On July 5 and 6 the Imperial Chancellor,

Bethmann Hollweg, the man in whom the constitution vested the sole responsibility, decided to take the risk and even over-trumped the Emperor when he threatened to weaken. That this was no "tragic doom," no "ineluctable destiny," but a deliberate decision of policy emerges beyond doubt from the diary of his private secretary, Kurt Riezler, who recorded in it his conversations with the Chancellor in the critical days (and, indeed, over many years). These diaries have not yet been published, but the extracts from them which have seen the light furnish irrefutable proof that during the July crisis Bethmann Hollweg was ready for war. More than this. Riezler's entry for the evening of July 8, after Bethmann Hollweg's return to Hohenfinow (where Rathenau was also stopping) shows what advance calculations the leaders of Germany were making in respect of the situation produced by the Sarajevo murder. According to his secretary, the Chancellor said: "If war doesn't come, if the Tsar doesn't want it or France panics and advises peace, we have still achieved this much, that we have manoeuvred the Entente into disintegration over this move."

In other words, Bethmann Hollweg reckoned with a major general war as the result of Austria's swift punitive action against Serbia. If, however, Russia and France were again to draw back (as in 1909 and 1911)—which he at first regarded as the less probable eventuality—then at least Germany would have achieved a signal diplomatic victory: she would have split Russia from France and isolated both without war. But war was what he expected, and how he expected its course to run we learn from his predecessor in the Chancellorship, Bülow, who had a long discussion with him at the beginning of August. Bethmann Hollweg told Bülow that he was reckoning with "a war lasting three, or at the most, four months . . . a violent, but short storm." Then, he went on, revealing his innermost wishes, it would "in spite of the war, indeed, through it," be possible to establish a friendly relationship with England, and through England with France. He hoped to bring about "a grouping of Germany, England and France against the Russia colossus which threatens the civilisation of Europe."

Bethmann Hollweg himself often hinted darkly during the war how closely Germany had been involved in the beginning of the war. He was less concerned with the "staging" of it than to register the spirit of the German leaders who had made it possible for the war to be begun even after the premises for it had collapsed. The following bitter words are taken from his address to the Central Committee of the Reichstag at the beginning of October, 1916, during the sharp debate on the initiation of unlimited submarine warfare; they outline Germany's real "guilt," her constant over-estimation of her own powers, and her misjudgment of realities:

"Since the outbreak of the war we have not always avoided the danger of underestimating the strength of our enemies. The extraordinary development of the last twenty years seduced wide circles into over-estimating our own forces, mighty as they are, in comparing them with those of the rest of the world . . . in our rejoicing over our own progress (we have) not paid sufficient regard to conditions in other countries."

The July crisis must not be regarded in isolation. It appears in its true light only when seen as a link between Germany's "world policy," as followed since the mid-1890s, and her war aims policy after August, 1914.

• • •

B. BETHMANN HOLLWEG'S SEPTEMBER MEMORANDUM

In retrospect it is easy to recognise in the Chancellor's war aims objectives of pre-war German economic ambitions in Belgium, Luxembourg and Lorraine, now directly incorporated in official policy but intensified by the Mitteleuropa idea and given an anti-British twist. These economic motives overshadowed the strategic and maritime aims which were designed finally to break the ring round "Fortress Germany," at the same time eliminating the two western great powers as future military opponents of Germany.

The realisation of this programme would have brought about a complete revolution in the political and economic power-relationships in Europe. After eliminating France as a great power, excluding British influence from the Continent and thrusting

Russia back, Germany purposed to establish her own hegemony over Europe. If we concede that it is a statesman's duty, even in the midst of armed conflict, to conceive and to set before himself a dispassionate and imaginative picture of the world at peace, again, we cannot but ask ourselves uneasily whether Bethmann Hollweg's picture could have provided an adequate foundation for an enduring peace in Europe. The realisation of his programme would have broken the coalition of the three Entente powers, but if their association had seemed irksome even in time of peace, what replaced it would have been an order so restricting the positions of the three great powers—Britain, France and Russia—and the freedom of manoeuvre of the smaller nations of Europe, as infallibly to lay up a store of terrible explosive material for new conflicts; especially as the federative element was to be subordinated to Prusso-Germany's claim to lead and dominate.

Bethmann Hollweg himself saw—he wrote as much to Delbrück on September 16, only a week after drawing up the programme, and while the effects of the check on the Marne were still unclear—that the formation of a great central European economic unit under German leadership "could not be brought about on the basis of agreement on common interests . . . but only under the pressure of political superiority, should we be in the position to dictate peace terms." The last part of this sentence shows that the Chancellor was already influenced by the reverse on the Marne. Nevertheless the special significance of the September Programme for the history of the development of Germany's intentions during the First World War lies in two points. First, it was no isolated inspiration of the Chancellor's: it represents the ideas of leading economic, political—and also military—circles. Secondly, the main ideas set forth in it remained, as we shall see, the essential basis of Germany's war aims right up to the end of the war, although modified from time to time to fit changing situations.

Finally, the Chancellor's ideas, far-reaching as they look to us today, were yet conceived as a programme of moderation, a check on the wave of annexationist feeling which had swept over all Germany after the military successes of August and September.

• • •

C. POPULAR PRESSURES

Like Gatzke, Fischer places much emphasis on the role of public opinion and pressure groups. His discussion of the annexationist views of the German academic community is both striking and depressing.

The outbreak of the World War and the popular excitement which this produced evoked stronger demands than ever before that Germany should make her weight felt in the world. Two decades of German "world policy" had generated and fostered in the German people a conviction that it was called, and entitled, to the status of a world power. A whole school of historians, the neo-Rankeists, had developed the theory of the rising system of world states, in which Germany would take her place as an equal, as she had in the old European state system. Beside the German historians stood an innumerable phalanx of publicists of the most various dispensations, who proclaimed the "German war" as Germany's occasion to rise from a great power to a world power. This idea first took shape in August, 1914, and then in the face of the difficulties which began to emerge in the winter of 1914–15 hardened into a fixed determination to fight the war through until the goal was reached.

THE "IDEAS OF 1914"

Behind this blend of national emotion and very purposeful political thought stood an intellectual movement, the product of German professors—both humanists and economists—who felt themselves called to provide the war with a positive philosophy. In the "Ideas of 1914," under which name this movement has gone down to history, the war was no longer merely a defensive struggle which Germany had to wage against the ring of enemies who had fallen on her, but something more than this: a higher, predestinate necessity rooted in the antithesis between the German spirit, German culture, German political forms, and the life and forms of her alien enemies. The disappointed hate-love towards Britain in particular swung round to unalloyed hatred of the British Empire. Britain, branded as the author of "encirclement," became the progenitor of all utilitarian, egotistical, purely mercenary powers; the Anglo-Saxon "shopkeepers' spirit" was contrasted with German "heroism." Meinecke talked of the lying phraseology of idealism which was used to mask a pure power policy, and of the danger to the development of any free personality presented by the "uniformalised, mechanical" Anglo-Saxon type of humanity. Britain was the old people, now abdicating its place in world history, Germany the young nation, strong, upsurging, only now fulfilling itself. The war was being waged to help this natural process to consummation. Germany would win the victory, not through fortune on the battlefield, but because she represented a higher culture fighting in the service of human history. The war became invested with a sort of religious nimbus; it appeared, not as a fight of one nation against another, most certainly not as a test of technical and economic potentials, but in the terms of Hegel and Ranke, as a struggle between contending moral forces.

This philosophic interpretation of the war—which had nothing to do with any realistic political thought—helped to mobilise German public opinion and released unsuspected reserves of force, precisely because of its non-rational, emotional appeal. This background explains both the war enthusiasm of the two first years of war and the 'nation's' claim to world power, with which the political and intellectual leaders of Germany identified themselves.

* * *

D. THE FORMULATION OF THE GERMAN PROGRAMME

Bethmann Hollweg had at first been reluctant to put Germany's war aims in writing and to communicate them to her allies, but had ended by giving way to Austrian pressure. Between November 4 and November 14, 1916, he held various conversations with the Emperor and with the Supreme Army

Command on war aims and on the text of a note to be sent to
Vienna. He began by sending the OHL, on November 4, a list of
war aims, and asking for the soldiers' comments. His list com-
prised five points:

(i) Recognition of the Kingdom of Poland.

(ii) Frontier rectifications through annexations of territory in
Courland and Lithuania, so that "counting in the future Kingdom of Poland, a good strategic frontier against Russia, running
from north to south, would be achieved."

(iii) In the west, guarantees in Belgium, "to be established, as
far as possible, through negotiations with King Albert." Should
it not prove possible to secure adequate guarantees, a strip of
land including Liége to be annexed.

(iv) French territory to be evacuated, except Longwy and
Briey; in return, France was to restore the lost parts of Alsace, or
to pay a war indemnity or compensation. Possibly also frontier
rectification in favour of France in Alsace.

(v) In respect of colonies, the proposals were either the restoration of the German colonies, except Kiaochow, the Carolines and
the Marianas, or "a general colonial settlement."

Hindenburg's reply arrived the next day. The general line of
the two drafts was the same, although Hindenburg's was the
more detailed and precise. Bethmann Hollweg accepted this
draft, although he softened it down somewhat in form when
passing it on to the Emperor and to Vienna, where it was handed
in on November 9.

On Point (i) the OHL has asked for frontier rectifications on
the Prussian-Polish frontier, the economic attachment of Poland
to Germany and 'influence over the Polish railway system' and
other economic *desiderata*—all points which had for years
figured, in whole or part, in the government's programme.

(ii) There was no difference in principle between the Chancellery and the OHL on the annexation of large areas of Courland and Lithuania; in particular, the Chancellor's programme
had included Vilno and Grodno since the spring of 1916. Hindenburg further wanted to include Brest-Litovsk, on the east
bank of the Bug, which was in any case to form the frontier
between the satellite state of Poland and Russia.

(iii) The OHL's detailed list of guarantees to be required from Belgium, use of the Campine coalfields, economic attachment to Germany, control of the Belgian railways, and a right of occupation, agreed exactly with the government's Belgian programme throughout the whole war. Finally, the Chancellor had told the Committee of the Federal Council only a few days before that, besides the acquisition of Liége, the dismantling of other fortresses and the right of passage in case of war might "perhaps" be "obtainable." There was only one of the soldiers' demands—a truly Utopian one—which the Chancellor rejected; they had asked for a war indemnity from Britain as compensation, in case Germany failed to obtain adequate occupation rights in Belgium.

(iv) Chancellor and Field-marshal were of one mind on the question of Longwy-Briey, only Hindenburg wanted, as Bethmann Hollweg had for two years, possible minor frontier rectifications in Alsace, not in favour of France but of Germany. In the final version Bethmann Hollweg gave way to Hindenburg on this point and also demanded war indemnities or compensation.

(v) The OHL wanted not only Germany's colonies back, but also the Congo state—the heart of Bethmann Hollweg's "Central African" plan.

(vi) The OHL further asked for compensation for the Germans outside the Reich and the entry of Luxemburg into the German Reich: a demand accepted by the Chancellor, if in somewhat veiled form, as "necessary in the event" of Germany's acquiring Longwy and Briey.

(vii) The November 9 version included further a "commercial treaty with Russia," which had not appeared in either Bethmann Hollweg's or the OHL's first list, but had figured prominently whenever war aims had been discussed in connection with the soundings for a separate peace, and a detailed draft of which had been prepared as early as the spring of 1916.

This last point shows that the apparently deep divergences between the political and military leaders resolve themselves, on closer inspection, into a difference of attitudes: the politicians' attitude was elastic, deliberately impenetrable and always at pains to keep a free hand; the soldiers' was hard, open, and intent on definition. The two parties were agreed in principle on Germany's war aims; the only question between them was whether and how far it was wise to bind their hands by communicating those aims to Germany's allies, her enemies, or a mediator.

But it was precisely this question of tactics in the proposed peace move that had to be discussed again between Germany and Austria-Hungary at the Berlin Conference of November 15 and 16. Burian had contented himself with expressing regret that the Germans were still refusing to publish their peace terms simultaneously with their peace offer—they would do no more than bring their terms with them to any peace negotiations; but he insisted obstinately that a binding joint programme of the four Central Powers' war aims must be drawn up in advance of the peace negotiations, and he finally got out of the Germans a hesitant and "academic" consent. The Germans' change of attitude when Wilson made his offer of mediation the next evening shows, however, that they wanted to avoid so binding themselves. One factor was certainly not only Burian's insistence on his own procedure, but also his criticisms of the substance of the German programme: he thought its demands in relation to France and Belgium too far-reaching and "hardly capable of realisation," and he was convinced that the possibilities of peace stood or fell with Germany's demands in the west. Bethmann Hollweg, for his part, criticised Austria's wishes in the Balkans as too far-reaching. He urged Burian not to "incorporate" Montenegro, except Lovčen and the coastal strip, in the Monarchy, but to let it join up with the new kingdom of Serbia which was to be established. Jagow and Zimmermann went further still; they wanted to give the kingdom an outlet to the sea at the expense of Albania. Jagow even raised the question "whether Albania might not be partitioned between Greece and Serbia." Serbia, thus enlarged and "strengthened economically, as far as possible," should then be made part of the Austro-Hungarian customs and economic system.

The remarks of the German statesmen, especially Jagow, reveal the outlines of a plan for the Balkans of which Jagow had spoken a year earlier, in November, 1915, and which took definite shape at a purely German conference on Balkan problems in May, 1917: an enlarged, economically strengthened Serbia was to be attached to Austria-Hungary and thus to Mitteleuropa as a new medium state, side by side with a friendly Bulgaria and a satellite Rumania, which was at that moment on the verge of accepting defeat and already marked down as an object of German economic interests. The partition of Albania would have meant the end of Burian's pet idea of establishing an Austrian protectorate over that country; on the other hand, the Germans proposed to draw Greece thereby into the German economic system, while between New Serbia and the enlarged Greece Germany would establish an outpost for her influence on the Adriatic in Valona, the chief port of Albania, which the German Admiralty was demanding as a naval base. This intrusion by Germany into Austria's most private sphere of interest reveals what was the position assigned to Austria-Hungary in Germany's plans for the future.

The Germans not only opposed Austria's wishes in the Balkans, but also refused to meet her most important demand for a guarantee of her territorial integrity, either in the shape of a joint war aims programme worked out between the four powers or, as the Austrians desired, by way of a declaration of solidarity between Germany and Austria-Hungary. Immediately after the publication of the Peace Offer of December 12, the Austrians pressed for the conclusion of a guarantee agreement to this effect. Bethmann Hollweg could not refuse altogether, but what he finally conceded, in order to pacify the Austrians, was no more than a gesture. In an *aide mémoire* which he read out to the Austro-Hungarian ambassador on December 21 and then handed over, he assured him that in the event of peace negotiations Germany would use the "pledges" of the occupied territories to use her influence in favour of the restoration of the Monarchy's former frontiers. This assurance did not, however, give Burian what he really wanted which was that the conclusion of peace should be made conditional on the restoration of the integrity of the Dual Monarchy.

● ● ●

E.   THE GERMAN-AUSTRIAN WAR
AIMS CONFERENCES OF MARCH, 1917

On March 16, 1917, four days after the success of the revolution in Russia, the long promised German-Austrian conference on war aims took place in Vienna. It has to be seen against the background of the Austro-French feelers, which had already been put out; not only was Count Mensdorff-Pouilly, the former Austro-Hungarian Ambassador in London, being sent to Switzerland, thence to spin threads towards France—this was all Bethmann Hollweg knew—but contact had already been made with Prince Sixtus of Parma. The Prince and his brother, who were nephews of the Empress Zita, were serving in the Belgian army and were prepared to act as intermediaries between the Emperor Charles and Poincaré. Czernin pinned great hopes on these conversations, since he realised plainly, and also stated unambiguously at the outset of the conference, that it was "entirely impossible" for Austria-Hungary to carry on the war longer than the coming autumn.

Czernin wanted to grasp France's "proffered hand," but Bethmann Hollweg was decidedly sceptical: France would make the cession of Alsace-Lorraine a *conditio sine qua non,* and that would mean a loss for Germany which he could not justify either to the Emperor or to the German people. Moreover, the occupied territories of France and Belgium must be kept as pledges for the return by Britain of the German colonies. The Chancellor therefore wanted the negotiator "to be strictly receptive and not to prejudice the future in any way." Unlike Czernin, he had hopes of the effects of the Russian revolution and of submarine warfare; that is, he still believed in the possibility of eventually concluding a separate peace on Germany's conditions.

Nevertheless Bethmann Hollweg made the motions of meeting Czernin's urgent wish that Germany's war aims should be reduced as nearly as possible to the maintenance of the *status quo* by pretending to the Austrian that Germany had now renounced far-reaching war aims against France. Czernin had proposed giving Mensdorff for his conversations a minimum and a maximum programme of the war aims of the Central Powers. The Chancellor gave him, as the maximum, the acquisition of Longwy-Briey without territorial counter-concessions by Germany, and as the minimum, "exchange of the Briey-Longwy ore fields against parts of Lorraine or Alsace." This was not Germany's "last word"—although the events of the turn of the year 1916–17 and later documents show that all Bethmann Hollweg thought of ceding was a few frontier villages. The "exchange" would have been quite illusory, especially as Belgium was excluded from the discussion.

In the east, the Chancellor simply took up the attitude of a conqueror. "Here," he told the Austrians, "so long as Germany is not defeated, all that can be considered is how much we take, how much we keep; at the worst, a return to the *status quo*." But even here, Bethmann Hollweg did not entirely disclose his cards to his closest ally; he clothed Germany's intention of dominating Congress Poland in the garb of Mitteleuropa. The establishment of the Kingdom of Poland would push eastward the Russian frontier in Central Europe, to the advantage of all the Central Powers. In that event Bethmann Hollweg was prepared "not to claim any Polish territory for Germany," i.e., to renounce annexing the Polish "Frontier Strip"; Germany would confine herself to strategically desirable acquisitions in Courland and Lithuania. The dimensions of the direct annexations—he explicitly named the governments of Grodno and Vilno—would, of course, depend on Germany's military position at the conclusion of peace. Should the Central Powers be forced to restore Congress Poland to Russia—if, that is, the general situation forced them to offer Russia a "cheap" peace—"then Germany would be thinking only of frontier rectifications on the Silesian and East Prussian frontiers"—that is, the Polish "Frontier Strip," as planned two years before.

Czernin's answer reflected the dilemma of the Dual Monarchy. He put the integrity of the Monarchy—in particular the recovery of East Galicia and the Bukovina—above the acquisition of Congress Poland. He thought it, however, impossible, on grounds of prestige, to let Germany acquire large territorial prizes (in Courland, Lithuania and Poland) and Bulgaria others, while the Monarchy "bleeding from a hundred wounds, came out empty-handed, or even diminished." He therefore proposed that at the end of the war "the territorial and economic gains should be brought into a certain agreement." He was evidently thinking of putting the war gains of all the Central Powers into a sort of common pool, out of which each partner should draw his share. To safeguard Austria-Hungary's interests he proposed partitioning Rumania on the lines sketched out in January, 1917.

Bethmann Hollweg and the Under-Secretary for Foreign Affairs, von Stumm, at once raised strong objections to Czernin's
proposal, announcing at the same time a new turn in Germany's
Rumanian policy. The Chancellor criticised the Austrian claim
to Rumania as giving the Danubian Monarchy an excessive share
of the spoils, and advocated instead preserving the kingdom of
Rumania as far as possible within its existing frontiers. He suggested that Austria might content herself with Western Wallachia, while Russia took, not the whole of Moldavia, but only
the northern tip of it. In these areas Germany was asking for
"nothing but economic advantages." Behind this apparent mod-
esty lay Germany's intention to secure for herself the hegemony
in Rumania, an aim which she pursued tenaciously, with many
changes of tactics, throughout 1917 and achieved in 1918 by the
Treaty of Bucharest.

Immediately after the session of March 16 Czernin set down
the proposals which he had made at the conference in even more
explicit form in a memorandum to the Emperor Charles: Germany must give up Alsace-Lorraine, in whole or part, and restore
Belgium; in return, she could keep Congress Poland. Austria
should cede the Trentino to Italy and receive compensation in
Rumania.

The renunciation of Poland was the central question discussed
at an Austro-Hungarian Common Ministerial Council, held on
March 22 under Charles' presidency, to consider Austria's position after the conference of the 16th. Emperor and Ministers
assumed that Germany was renouncing any territorial gains in
the west. On this assumption, the ministers present were prepared to reserve the east for their allies as "compensation" and
"as a logical consequence" to renounce their own aspirations in
Poland. When we know that only two days earlier the Emperor
had drawn up with his cousin the so-called "first Sixtus letter"
to Poincaré, promising that Charles would "support the just
claim of France to recover Alsace-Lorraine with all means at
his disposal and with all the personal influence he could exert
on his ally," and would call on Germany to reinstate Belgium
as a sovereign state with its colonies, we can realise how compul-
sively necessary the Austrians felt it to be to persuade their German ally to make renunciations in the west and thus somehow

or other make peace. At this council the Austrians for the first time mentioned as a war aim of their own the inclusion, already suggested by Germany in November, 1916, of a diminished Serbia within the customs area of the Danubian Monarchy.

Meanwhile the effects of the Russian revolution seemed to call for another meeting between the allies. It took place in Berlin on March 26–27. The exchange of Poland against the lion's share of Rumania was confirmed, although Austria stipulated that if the Entente refused to allow Rumania to be partitioned, she could not renounce Poland. Czernin, however, linked the Polish and Rumanian questions with that of Mitteleuropa, for which Germany was pressing strongly, by stipulating that both German hegemony over Congress Poland (which would also necessarily carry with it the inclusion of Poland in the German Customs Union) and the resumption of economic negotiations on the Mitteleuropa project should be conditional on Wallachia going to the Danubian Monarchy.

On principle Czernin was anxious that the Central Powers should not exclude the possibility of peace with either west or east by pitching their demands too high. Bethmann Hollweg, however, invoked German public opinion to insist most obstinately on Germany's war aims in the west, saying that to accept the *status quo* either in Belgium or in Longwy–Briey would be "a very heavy sacrifice" for Germany. He insisted even more strongly on Germany's war aims in the east, although he said that he might make far reaching concessions, especially towards Russia, as price for a separate peace.

The results of these two conferences were committed to paper in the shape of a short resumé signed by Bethmann Hollweg and Czernin jointly on March 27. The two men agreed firstly on a minimum programme which made the evacuation of any occupied enemy territory "primarily" dependent on recognition of the territorial *status quo* of both powers in both east and west. This programme, which was however to apply only in the case of a relatively unfavourable issue to the war, was more advantageous to Austria-Hungary, which would have recovered East Galicia and the Bukovina, whereas Germany would have got back only a few villages, since no German territory was in enemy occupation except a small corner of Alsace. More instructive for the history of Germany's war aims is the maximum programme, which was to apply if the war ended favourably. For this eventuality, for which Germany was putting out all her strength, the resumé laid down a framework which was elastic in two directions and amounted to another success for the German standpoint: if the Austrians had talked in Vienna of "a certain agreement" and even of "an automatic equalisation" in the division of the spoils of war, they now had to accept the German *fiat* that "the territorial acquisitions of the two Powers must be made proportionate to the achievements of each." Acceptance of military efficiency as the criterion for the division of the spoils at the end of the war could only work in Germany's favour, since the German troops were undoubtedly bearing the brunt of the war effort of the Central Powers, in the east as well as the west; German forces had played by far the greater part, even in the conquests of Serbia and Rumania. Finally, the resumé also indirectly left Germany a free hand in the west. While Austria's territorial gains were to be "primarily in Rumania," Germany was to get acquisitions "chiefly in the east"—thus partly also in the west.

THE KREUZNACH WAR AIMS
PROGRAMME OF APRIL 23, 1917

The Chancellor obviously cannot have informed the OHL of the Vienna agreements, and the Foreign Ministry and Bethmann Hollweg's own successor afterwards showed themselves unaware of the existence of the document. Consequently, when the Austrian Emperor and Empress, with Count Czernin, came to Bad Homburg on April 3, the OHL pressed for an Austro-German conference to define the war aims of both states. The military thought it necessary for the German military and political authorities to meet beforehand to discuss Germany's war aims between themselves. Bethmann Hollweg again opposed a fixed programme of war aims, because he thought it would hamper possible negotiations for a separate peace with either France or Russia. On April 16 he again said that the unaltered aim of his policy was to break the enemy coalition, if possible, even to draw one of the former enemies over to Germany's side.

Pressed by Hindenburg to define Germany's war aims, the

Chancellor replied that he was informed of the wishes of the OHL and the naval staff from their memoranda of the previous December, and meant "to achieve the very utmost possible of those demands which are directed towards increasing our military security." The Chancellor further declared himself ready to subordinate general political and economic considerations to military ones, thus giving the military priority over the civilian in the matter of war aims. From this point onwards he found it very difficult to oppose even the exaggerated annexationist demands of the OHL. Nor was this all. He lost even such limited freedom of action as had been left him in the discussion of war aims when Hindenburg and Holtzendorff, mistrusting him, went to the Emperor at General Headquarters and got him to order the Chancellor on April 20 to draw up a specific war aims programme, with maximum and minimum demands, in view of the possibility of peace with Russia and of the approaching negotiations with Austria-Hungary. The Emperor also prejudged an important issue in the sense desired by the OHL by laying down, in respect of Lithuania, that for strategic reasons Vilno, Kovno and Grodno were in no case to be allowed to go to Poland.

On April 20 the Emperor told Bethmann Hollweg to come to Kreuznach on the 23rd for the big debate on war aims. The necessity of producing a war aims programme agreed between the government and the OHL could no longer be evaded. On the 21st Bethmann Hollweg held a strictly secret conference with the inner ring of the Prussian Ministry of State, preparatory to the meeting. At this meeting Helfferich, in agreement with the Chancellor, produced the new formula of "autonomy," which was to be applied in the areas which Germany had hitherto proposed to "annex," viz., Lithuania, Courland, Livonia and now Estonia also.

The Kreuznach Conference was attended by the Imperial Chancellor, Zimmerman, Hindenburg, Ludendorff and the head of the Political Section of the Government-General in Brussels, von der Lancken. The minutes of this meeting were published shortly after the war, but have hitherto been taken too much in isolation and regarded as a specific expression of the German military's annexationist ambitions. It is true that the formulation of war aims reached at this conference was primarily dictated by the wishes of the OHL, but a survey of the development of Germany's war aims from Bethmann Hollweg's programme of September, 1914, to the visible unfolding and realisation of Germany's wishes in the east at Brest-Litovsk reveals not only continuity of intention but also general agreement in principle between the military and civilian authorities.

• • •

The sum of these demands leaves on the reader who surveys them in retrospect the same impression as they made at the time on Admiral von Müller, the Chief of the Naval Staff: "My impression: completely immoderate, in east and west alike." These war aims could, of course, only be realised if Germany was in a position to dictate the peace as victor. Bethmann Hollweg expressly pointed this out immediately after the conference in a minute which did not go outside the Foreign Ministry; he declared himself not obliged to continue the war, under all circumstances, until these aims should have been achieved. In this minute the Chancellor took exactly the same line as in his letter to Hindenburg of April 16, in which he had admitted the primacy of the military war aims, as he did at the conference, but refused to commit himself finally. The special significance and meaning of this reservation related to the feelers which were being put out by Erzberger at the same time for a separate peace with Russia.

The criterion for the appreciation of Germany's war aims policy is the intention to realise as much of these aims as the military situation and any unavoidable consideration for her allies allowed, not how much tactical freedom the Chancellor enjoyed in his pursuit of them.

The primacy of Germany's own war aims over those of her allies was confirmed immediately after Kreuznach by Zimmermann, when he opposed categorically a suggestion that a conference of all four Central Powers should be convoked to define their war aims. "Such joint conferences," he wrote, "jeopardise the realisation of our own war aims, and it is of those that we must think first." He therefore said that the first step—which would be hard enough—should be to reach an understanding with Austria-Hungary alone, through normal diplomatic channels; only afterwards should discussions be opened with Bulgaria and Turkey.

When, then, the Kreuznach Conference is viewed in its historic context, it becomes plain that what Hans Herzfeld calls its "terrifying list" of proposed annexations is no isolated testimony to the greed of the German military. Its programme fits smoothly into the list of war aims discussions and programmes which preceded and followed it.

•   •   •

F. THE TREATY OF BREST-LITOVSK

The Peace of Brest-Litovsk is undoubtedly one of the most important political events in which Germany herself took a direct and active part between the outbreak and the end of the war. Judgments on the "forgotten peace" range between condemnation of it as a peace of force, as foreign critics saw it at the time, and the ebullient praise given to it by Wilhelm II as one of the "greatest successes of world history, whose significance only our grandchildren will truly appreciate." The broadest circles of German public opinion agreed with the Emperor, and German Protestantism, or at least one of its leading organs, saw in the triumph of Germany's sword over Russia a sort of divine judgment in favour of Germany's cause in general. Here is what the *Allgemeine Evangelisch-Lutherische Kirchenzeitung* wrote:

"Peace without annexations or indemnities! So men resolve. The slogan was coined by Germany's enemies when Germany's sword grew too heavy for them. The wolves wanted to escape unpunished for having ranged abroad, spilt German blood, ravaged German prosperity and inflicted wounds which will be long in healing. What was to remain was to be an impoverished, diminished Reich on which anyone thereafter could wreak his will . . . but here, too, God willed otherwise. He made Russia's masters drink of the cup of madness, so that they fell like robbers on their own peoples, until the latter at last called for German help. And out of the same cup drank the Russian negotiators, who fooled all the world and at last thought up the master stroke of breaking off the negotiations. That was God's hour. Germany's armies pressed on, took city after city, land after land, everywhere greeted as liberators. And Russia, who wanted to give no indemnities, was forced at the last minute to yield up uncountable booty: 800 locomotives, 8,000 railway trucks with every kind of treasure and supply; God knew that we needed it. And we also needed guns and munitions for the last blow against the enemy in the west. God knew that too. So He freely gave us, since God is rich, 2,600 guns, 5,000 machine guns, two million shells for the artillery, rifles, aircraft, lorries, and innumerable other things. . . . England and France had paid for it and made it, Germany received it. Only when Russia had given all that up, was she allowed and indeed compelled to make peace. Thus it was decided by God, a true Peace of God, contrary to everything that men had planned and wanted. Whatever may happen to the liberated border states, Russia will never get them back, and the protection and support which they seek they will find in Germany."

A later generation may look on such a paragraph as a piece of hysteria and an abuse of religion. It cannot, however, be denied that it reflects what was in the spring of 1918 the feeling of a great majority of the politically dominant classes of Germany —and it is only they who matter when we consider Germany's policy in the war.

After 1919 the Allies often retorted to German criticisms of the Treaty of Versailles by pointing to the ruthless severity of the Peace of Brest-Litovsk. By that time German public opinion had come to regard the treaty more soberly. In view of Germany's political situation new judgments were almost always apologias, and they have coloured German historiography up to the present day. One of the most important participants on the German side, General Hoffmann, has, for example, replied to all critics of the treaty in his memoirs, which appeared in 1929, by pointing out that the Allies technically annulled the German–Russian Treaty at Versailles, but used the situation created by Germany as the basis for their re-organisation of eastern Europe when they set up the ring of states nicknamed the *cordon sanitaire*.

It is also often pointed out that the Brest-Litovsk Treaty did not take away a single square yard of ethnically Russian territory,

so that they cannot be held up as examples of German annexationism. Kühlmann used this argument as early as January 23,
1918, when pleading the case for the treaty before the Central
Committee of the Reichstag, and we still hear it today. In each
case the argument is seductive because it is, technically, absolutely correct. If, however, we are to reach a correct and just appreciation of the whole problem of Brest-Litovsk, we need to
relate later events as they emerged after the collapse of Germany
in November, 1918 with Germany's actual aims. Then what we
have said, and what innumerable documents in the German
archives confirm, can leave no doubt that Germany's aim was
not to confer independence and national liberty on Poland,
Lithuania, Courland, Livonia, Estonia and the Ukraine, but on
the contrary to fetter them closely to the German Reich and to
Mitteleuropa by treaties which were only nominally international and by personal unions, economic and customs unions,
and military conventions. "Germany as the power of order in
East-Central Europe" regarded the separation from Russia of
all these countries, and also of Finland and later of Georgia, only
as a means of thrusting Russia back and extending Germany's
sphere of power far eastward.

Furthermore, German policy towards Russia did not even stay
within the limits marked out at Brest-Litovsk. In the summer of
1918 it reached out far beyond these limits, as far as the Caucasus.
In a message to the Hetman of the Don Cossacks Wilhelm II
elaborated a regular plan of dividing Russia, after Poland, the
Baltic provinces and the Caucasus had been detached from her,
into four independent states: the Ukraine, the South-Eastern
League (the anti-Bolshevik district between the Ukraine and the
Caspian), Central Russia, and Siberia.

The Treaty of Brest-Litovsk brought no real peace in the east.
Strong German forces had to be left in the east to maintain the
situation created at Brest-Litovsk and afterwards, and these could
not be used for the decisive battles in the west. But politically
the most serious consequence of Brest-Litovsk was its effect on
the western allies, and in particular on the attitude and feelings
of President Wilson. He had already been disappointed by Hertling's rejection of his Fourteen Points, and he saw in the Peace
of Brest-Litovsk proof that there was in Germany no opposition
to a policy based purely on power and self-interest. What disap-

pointed him most was the attitude of the German Majority Socialists, for he had thought to see in them a liberal oppositional
party and the kernel of a democratic Germany. Now they had,
as he saw it, submitted to the policy of "autocracy" by abstaining
on the vote. It was only after this episode that he dropped all
hesitation and mobilised every resource to help the Allies defeat
monarchic-military Germany.

• • •

G. IMPERIUM GERMANICUM

A survey of Germany's aims at the beginning and in the middle of 1918, when German self-confidence was at its peak in the
expectation of early victory, discloses a picture of an *imperium*
of grandiose dimensions. In the west: Belgium, Luxemburg,
Longwy–Briey linked with Germany on such terms as to make
possible the adherence of France and Holland and to isolate
Britain and force her to recognise Germany's position; in the
east: Courland, Livonia, Estonia and Lithuania, from Reval to
Riga and Vilno, the Polish Frontier Strip and Rump Poland all
closely fettered to Germany; in the south-east: Austria-Hungary
clamped into Germany as a cornerstone, then Rumania and Bulgaria, and beyond them the Ottoman Empire as an object of
Germany's Asiatic policy. Command of the eastern Mediter-
ranean was to compel the adherence of Greece and secure the
route through Suez, while the domination of the Black Sea guaranteed the economic mastery of the Ukraine, the Crimea and
Georgia, and the command of the Baltic compelled Sweden and
Finland, with their riches, to take the German side. On top of
all this was the position of at least economic hegemony in Rump
Russia.

The counterpart overseas of this European extended basis—
Mitteleuropa surrounded by a ring of vassal states—was to be
the central African colonial empire safeguarded by naval bases
and linked with the Near East through the Sudan and Suez.
With this economic and political power in Africa, reinforced by
the command of the strategic and technical key-points on the
route to South America to expand and consolidate the strong
economic interests already established there before the war, Ger-

many was to make herself a colonial and economic power of world status. Yet concentration on the African empire implied no withdrawal from the eastern hemisphere. Germany was maintaining her interests in Samoa and New Guinea and trying to initiate in China a more elastic policy, confined purely to the safeguarding of her economic interests. Above all, she hoped that by ceding Kiaochow to Japan she would be able to renew her old connections with that country against both Russia and the Anglo-Saxon powers.

Germany's political and economic *imperium* would have represented a concentration of force far surpassing Bismarck's empire in resources and human material. The old industrial areas of the Ruhr and Luxemburg, the Saar, German Lorraine, Saxony and Upper Silesia were to be reinforced by French Lorraine, Belgium, Poland and Bohemia. For her supply of ore, besides her own production and the assured imports from Sweden, she could have drawn on the ores of Austria, Poland, Longwy–Briey, the Ukraine, the Caucasus, Turkey and Katanga. To the oil of Galicia was added that of Rumania, the Caucasus and Mesopotamia, to her own agricultural production that of the Balkans and the north-east, to her previous imports from her old colonies in Africa, the abundant produce of central Africa; markets previously contested would be replaced by near-monopoly in Georgia, Turkey, Russia, the Ukraine, the Balkans, the north-east, the north and the west. The weight of the German Reich in matters of commercial policy would unquestionably have put Germany in an impregnable position of world-economic power. The economic agreements were, moreover, to be safeguarded by military treaties.

Military conventions with Finland, the Baltic states, Lithuania, Poland, the Ukraine, Georgia, Turkey, Bulgaria, Rumania and Austria-Hungary, and in a negative sense also with Belgium, had been planned, and most of them at least initialled. Through these economic, political and military links Germany would have created a European bloc which would have put her on a level with the three world powers of America, Britain and—if she could still be counted—Russia, and have given her a rank far above that of any European power of the old days.

The realisation of this world-wide aim depended on victory in the west, where the fresh and unexhausted power of America had come to the assistance of the British, French and Belgian armies.

32 FROM *Gerhard Ritter*
The Political Role of Bethmann Hollweg during the First World War

The late Professor Gerhard Ritter, at the time of his death in 1967 the dean of German historians and the most distinguished representative of the more traditionalist and nationalist German historians, strongly opposed Professor Fischer's views in a series of articles and in the last two volumes of his monumental study, Staatskunst und Kriegshandwerk *("The Art of Statesmanship and the Craft of War"). Ritter was particularly insistent on defending Bethmann Hollweg, whom he viewed as a victim of immoderate generals and of public demands for annexations. Thus, the moderate statesman Bethmann Hollweg is seen as the opponent of military technicians and radical annexationists. Furthermore, insofar as Bethmann did support annexations or indemnities, he did so to win security for Germany and to break through the circle of enemies surrounding the Fatherland. The selection below is taken from Professor Ritter's report at the International Congress of Historical Sciences in Vienna in 1965. It is followed by excerpts from Fritz Fischer's reply and the comment of the Austrian historian, Dr. Fritz Fellner.*

The character and political attitude of the German Imperial Chancellor Theobold von Bethmann Hollweg has only most recently been made the object of thorough study on the basis of the sources. . . .

In traditional historical writing Bethmann Hollweg appears as the representative of a moderate foreign policy, who was steering toward a peace of understanding based on the renunciation of far reaching goals of conquest, but who was unable to suc-

SOURCE (32). Translated by the editor from Gerhard Ritter, "Die politische Rolle Bethman Hollwegs waehrend des ersten Weltkrieges," in *Comité International des Sciences Historiques*, XII Congres International des Sciences Historiques, Vienna, 29 Août–5 Septembre 1965 (Horn/Wien, Verlag Ferdinand Berger & Söhne, 1965), IV, Rapports, pp. 271–278 and Remarks of Fritz Fischer and F. Fellner, *ibid.*, V, Actes, pp. 721–725, 746–748.

ceed in this endeavor against the opposition of annexationists, Pan-Germans and militarists. Surprisingly, (Fritz) Fischer believes that he is able to demonstrate from the documents of Bethmann's time in office, that in his political planning he distinguished himself from the boundless annexationism of a Ludendorff "only in extent, form and method," but not in substance. He is supposed to have held with the greatest stubbornness until his fall in June 1917 to an annexationist war aims program which he formulated on September 9, 1914 at the height of German military success in France. In the presentation of Fischer, this appears as the logical expression of a striving for power which is supposed to have dominated German foreign policy and economic policy well before 1914. . . .

The so-called "war aims program" of September 9, 1914 is contained in a memorandum, which Bethmann sent from the imperial headquarters to his deputy in Berlin, State Secretary Delbrück. In it, the imperial authorities were called upon to prepare a list of the most pressing demands of Germany for the peace negotiations which might soon be beginning, and there was already sketched out in brief summary form what the Chancellor himself at the moment considered to be especially desirable. . . .

The memorandum unquestionably demonstrates that Bethmann, at the high point of German military success in France shortly before the reversal on the Marne, did not remain untouched by the powerful current of extravagant hopes for victory which overwhelmed the German nation at that time and which did not intend to remain satisfied with a mere maintenance of the *status quo ante bellum* in the case of a total victory for Germany. He wanted to use such a victory for a substantial improvement of Germany's situation in Europe—no differently than the statesmen on the other side desired for their own countries in that they similarly began to forge far-reaching war aims programs in the fall of 1914 and even set them down in international agreements beginning in the spring of 1915. On the other hand, the memorandum of Bethmann appears only as the first, temporary consideration of what was desirable, not as the final formulation of unconditional demands, and therefore not as a "war aims program." The Chancellor never publicly committed himself to it. In his Reichstag speeches until his fall he had consciously avoided making any concrete formulation of "war aims," and to be sure with the express intention of maintaining a free hand for negotiations according to the military situation as soon as an attainable possibility presented itself— a free hand for negotiation with the enemy, but also a free hand over against the German parties and popular currents, for he did not want to be drawn into the passionately fought opposition between annexationists and anti-annexationists, between extreme hopes for victory and desires for conquest, on the one side, and resignation and self-denial, on the other side. Rather, for as long as possible, he sought to prevent open discussion of the so-called war aims question entirely out of the justified concern that it would lead to a deep, incurable division of the nation in the middle of war.

Fischer naturally also knows something about these efforts. But he believes that he is able to demonstrate from the study of the secret memoranda and correspondence of the Foreign Office and Reich Chancellery that the Chancellor, in his basic political position, tended toward the side of the annexationists, even if he hid this more or less from the public in order not to lose the support of the right wing of the Social Democrats. Also, he is to have continuously operated under illusions about Germany's chances of victory until his fall—so much so, that he actually sabotaged the promising, frequently reiterated American offers of mediation. He only permitted his own peace offer of December 12, 1916 to be made because he wanted thereby to anticipate a mediatory action by Wilson and prepare diplomatically for unrestricted submarine warfare.

I believe that I have demonstrated the opposite in my book from the same sources. Even the so-called September Program which Fischer discovered is, in my view, misinterpreted if it is understood as a "grasp for world power." It only demonstrates the Chancellor's intention of forcefully destroying the ring of enemy alliances which had threatened the Central Powers for a long time and which had permitted Austria's Balkan war to become a European war, and thereby to establish certain "securities" and "guarantees" for the future of Germany. Naturally one can interpret every effort of this kind as a striving for "world rule," but I believe that I have shown that Bethmann himself understood his plan only as a more expanded form of defence.

One would certainly have to ask if the means which he considered at the time, especially keeping open the door to France through Belgium and keeping the latter in submission as a form of vassal state, would not have created the germ of new wars instead of "security." Bethmann himself was not entirely comfortable with this, as can be demonstrated from private utterances even in 1914. And he was completely clear about the fact that one could never think about peace negotiations with England without the liberation and restoration of Belgium. Thus time and time again he sought after possibilities of finding a way which would satisfy Belgium's need for freedom and sovereignty and Germany's need for security. He negotiated with King Albert of Belgium by irregular channels since the winter of 1915–16 and, as I could demonstrate from Belgian source material, he seems to have gone very far in his offers. It is a demonstrable error of Fischer when he argues that the negotiations broke down because of the enormity of German war aims. It is correct that Bethmann always avoided a *public* declaration to the effect that Germany would completely liberate, restore and compensate Belgium. But the reason for this was not a boundless quest for power and conquest, but the conviction that Belgium would never again be satisfied with a formal guarantee of her neutrality through the great powers after the horrors of the invasion but would probably seek a military alliance with the western powers. In the case of a new war, however, that meant deployment of the enemy forces near Aachen, no longer at the Belgian-French border, but rather in close proximity to the German industrial region on the lower Rhine. Bethmann believed he needed some kind of "guarantee" against this. But how could he bring this about if he publicly declared Germany's complete renunciation of Belgium without any certainty that he could negotiate about a moderate peace in exchange—all this leaving aside the loud protests which were to be expected from German public opinion? Such certainty, however, never existed during his term in office. If one reproaches him therefore for his all-too-cautious remarks on the Belgian question, one has to make similar reproaches against the Entente governments who never considered declaring their readiness to negotiate without prior evacuation of France and Belgium, surrender of Alsace-Lorraine to France, and thorough destruction of Prusso-German military power. It is a very notable deficiency of Fischer's book that one finds practically nothing about this in it. He also remains silent about the fact that the Chancellor practically gave up the plan for a "central European economic alliance" under German leadership in October 1914 and that in a discussion with Pan-German politicians in December of the same year he declared that he would prefer not to annex a single quadrameter of French territory, that France was Germany's most noble opponent and that he himself did not want to tear open any new wounds between the two lands since those of 1870–71 still had not healed.

Between this declaration and the so-called September Program lay the reversal on the Marne and a profoundly sobering discussion with the Chief of the General Staff, Von Falkenhayn, who told him bluntly in the middle of November that one could no longer think of a total German victory if one did not succeed in making a separate peace with at least one of the enemies, perhaps Russia. Bethmann took this very seriously and in a note to the Foreign Office immediately thereafter stated that he himself would view a peace on the basis of the status quo as a great success because then Germany still would have maintained herself against half the world, but that the German people probably would not be satisfied with it. With this one touches upon the greatest and most fateful difficulty of the Reich Chancellor's policy. He no longer believed in a German victory in the full sense of the word, but if he did not want simply to capitulate, then he had to spur on the German people and his allies to hold out bravely until the enemy was driven to the limits of their strength in a war of exhaustion and a peace of understanding thereby became possible. But that meant that he must now as before let confidence in victory stream forth in his speeches. Only in this way could he hold the allies on Germany's side, and only in this way could he hope to secure a Reichstag majority in support of war credits. It is self-understood that a war so filled with enormous sacrifices as that of 1914, the first total war in modern history, would release in Germany as in the lands of her opponents great patriotic excitement and along with it excessive, largely fantastic war aims desires. To have thrown himself against this wave of excited hopes for victory and desires of conquest openly and with all his energy would not only have endangered the Chancellor's chances of parliamentary success, but would most probably have led to his downfall. For the Kaiser, whose confidence was the Chancellor's only support, was even without this continually pressured by Bethmann's reactionary and militaristic opponents to let him go. Should he have risked it? To give way before these enemies would have been to allow Germany to move along a very dangerous course. Since the fall of 1916 the most dangerous of his enemies was the ruthless iron-willed General Ludendorff, the all powerful "chief" of the Supreme Command, who understood how to systematically introduce the latter into political decisions.

So Bethmann Hollweg very quickly found himself pressed between contrary currents which increasingly narrowed the amount of freedom of decision available to him and often simply compelled him to cautious evasion instead of clear and forceful decision making. Only when one penetrates deeply into the intricacies of this situation can one be fair to his political performance in general, and it is one of the greatest failures of Fischer's book that the reader receives no satisfactory conception of the difficult political situation of the Chancellor. Thus Fischer uses the fantastic war aims program which the Supreme Command pushed through with the Kaiser on April 23, 1917 to demonstrate that Bethmann, who signed it out of necessity, hardly differed from Ludendorff in his annexationist goals—but he (Fischer) says nothing about the important formal minute for the record of the Chancellor, which practically robbed his signature of all value and the fact that it was just the object of the Supreme Command on April 23 to demonstrate to the Kaiser the need to dismiss Bethmann. The eastern policy of Bethmann Hollweg is similarly presented in a one-sided manner: one learns, to be sure, that since the end of 1916 he gave way more and more to the pressure of almost all of German public opinion which stormily demanded the annexation of Courland and Lithuania or at least a protectorate over these areas. But one does not learn that on June 15, 1915 he expressly asked the Chief of the General Staff to oppose all plans for annexation in the Baltic among the higher officers because they would seriously burden the future relationship with Russia, and just as little do we learn that he pursued the organization of Poland under German protection only very much against his will (for reasons of a very complicated kind which cannot be discussed here) and that it was actually

Ludendorff who ruined Germany's Polish policy by overhaste, while Bethmann was adamantly decided—also in 1917—in no case to allow peace with Russia to be ruined because of German territorial conquests in the East.

Finally, it is the exact opposite of the truth that he fundamentally opposed Wilson's peace mediation. The only thing that is correct is that he worked against a direct interference of America in the question of the conditions of peace—and to be sure because (with good reason) he feared that the negotiating position of Germany's enemies would be greatly strengthened by it since Wilson stood completely on the side of England in his sympathies and prejudices. Once begun, the peace negotiations could only have been broken off over individual questions with the greatest difficulty. On the other hand, since the spring of 1916 the Chancellor continuously strove with enthusiasm and persistence to bring Wilson in as a peace mediator in the sense that he (Wilson) should bring the Allies to the negotiating table with the Germans. He was also firmly convinced that he would be able to bring Kaiser William to give up immoderate demands as soon as there was finally a hint of serious prospects for peace. His enthusiasm was all the greater because he fully understood that he would only be in a position to prevent unrestricted submarine warfare in the long run if he could open up to the Kaiser and the military concrete prospects for a peace of understanding. It was for this reason that he had the peace offer of the Central Powers sent forth on December 12, 1916 without waiting any longer for Wilson's action—not in order to anticipate the latter, but rather because there was the greatest danger of simply being overrun by the military and naval leadership. That he left out concrete details concerning the war aims of the Central Powers in this peace offer demonstrates in no way that this offer was not meant seriously. Rather it can be demonstrated that, on the one hand, he had to fear making known the very far reaching aims of the allies, above all Bulgaria, before the beginning of the negotiations, and on the other hand, he had to avoid mobilizing German public opinion and the German Supreme Command against himself by revealing his own, very modest minimal program before the entire world. Ludendorff and Hindenburg would have opposed such a peace offer with their entire authority.

The offer was therefore hopeless from the beginning—but also because the other side gave no thought at all to entering into negotiations without the complete defeat of Germany. Since they also said this openly, they struck from the Chancellor's hand every possibility of preventing the unrestricted employment of the "wonder weapon," the U-Boat, against England, which was stormily demanded by the Supreme Command, the naval leadership and the majority of the Reichstag deputies and which was generally regarded as the last but also certain means of compelling this most unreachable of Germany's enemies to give in. He was himself clear that the entry of America into the ranks of our enemies would thereby become unavoidable—something which he, in contrast to the leaders of public opinion, regarded as fateful. It is probably true that the initially unexpected success of the U-Boats in March and April 1917 and the unexpected speedy collapse of the great spring offensive of the French at the same time seems to have reduced his pessimism somewhat for a time. But it is completely misleading to maintain that he was filled with confidence of victory and therefore gave in to the annexationist demands of the Supreme Command. If that were so, then that latter would not have needed to have used a well organized intrigue to rob him of his parliamentary support so that a Hindenburg and Ludendorff ultimatum could then bring him down.

All in all, one confronts the moving tragedy of a statesman, whose sincere desire to end the war with a reasonable adjustment of power instead of through a peace of force is not to be doubted, but who was denied success, not simply and not primarily through certain defects of his nature (like slowness of decision and the tendency toward painstaking reflection), but rather through an excess of external hinderances and highly effective counterforces as well as through the weaknesses of his constitutional position. I view Fischer's total conception of his policy after all this to be misconceived, and I can only explain this by the fact that this historian, overwhelmed by the enormous amount of source material, failed to place himself in the position of those who were acting at the time with the necessary patience and concern. To this obviously must be added the influence of certain politically fashionable currents in Germany today, to whom every form of German great power politics, even in the age of European imperialism, appears simply condemnable. The feverishly increased activity of German wartime politics as Fischer encountered it in the mass of documents apparently became sinister to him. Its restless effort to shatter the tsarist control over non-Russian nationalities in Russia, to incite revolutionary movements among the Russian peasantry, to undermine the British Empire in the Near East, to strengthen the forces of revolution within France—all this he prematurely describes as a striving for German domination of the world instead of as measures of political conflict in the most extreme emergency. In the process he also often introduces certain extreme war aims of the last year of the war, the period of Ludendorff's political supremacy, into the period of Bethmann Hollweg's government. To this must be added that the large amount of literature based on sources of modern American research on Wilson and his advisers is apparently only inadequately known to him so that he overestimates the chances of the mediation efforts of Wilson and his friend House considerably. In short, leaving aside the service provided by opening up an enormous collection of unpublished source material, I believe that Fischer's book is lacking in full maturity and that his theses will not be able to be sustained for long in the realm of scientific scholarly history.

• • •

33 REPLY BY   *Fritz Fischer*
                      (Hamburg)

1. Gerhard Ritter is concerned with the personality of the Chancellor Bethmann Hollweg; he is motivated by a biographical interest, as the title . . . of the Rapport before us shows. Germany and its problems come in only secondarily. . . . For me, in line with western as well as eastern European historical writing, the concern is the political-structural, social-economic and religious-cultural foundations of the forces determining the policy of the German Empire. The question of what Bethmann Hollweg wanted is not so important for me as the question of what he could do or had to do. Bethmann Hollweg himself described his domestic as well as his foreign policy as a policy of the diagonal. The direction of a diagonal is determined—for that is the law of the parallelogram—by the strength of com-

ponent forces which stand opposed to it, i.e., translated into historical-political terms, Bethmann Hollweg's policy of the diagonal—as he himself said—was more determined by the forces of the imperialist, military, conservative and national-liberal Germany than by the much weaker democratic-socialist forces. . . .

2. Ritter places at the center of his presentations Bethmann Hollweg's contributions to efforts for a separate peace and for a peace of understanding. But he is compelled to admit that Bethmann Hollweg only undertook this goal after—as Ritter says—the "reversal" at the Marne, or better said, the German defeat on the Marne. . . . Yet the Marne was only the beginning of military defeats: the very costly battles in Flanders at Arras, Ypres, Langemark had to follow before Moltke's successor, Falkenhayn (who still hoped to force victory with the use of newly formed reserve corps, composed in part of student volunteers) had to resignedly declare, "The army is a shattered instrument." But with a shattered instrument a "total victory"—as Ritter describes the German goal—was no longer attainable. Thus Falkenhayn's demand for a separate peace with one of the three enemies. He proposed Russia, a demand which Bethmann Hollweg accepted in his letter to Zimmermann, his and Jagow's representative in the Foreign Office in Berlin on November 18. To now strive for a separate peace in order to save what was possible to save from the effort which failed and at least to get a "respectable" peace with two of the enemies was no demonstration of the insight of a great statesman but rather a bitter necessity as a consequence of the previous overestimation of one's own strength. (In the process Ritter leaves out of consideration how Bethmann Hollweg wanted to see the separate peace as a political calculation. A separate peace appeared to him as the one possibility of breaking the phalanx of the allied enemies . . . without thereby giving up the original goals. . . .

When Gerhard Ritter presents the so-called "peace of understanding" through a "war of exhaustion" (thus a war in which the others would be so exhausted that they would be ready for an understanding) as the actual and, so to speak, profoundly virtuous goal of Bethmann Hollweg, then one must say in reply, that this was just the type of war which Germany did not want to conduct and could not conduct and for whose avoidance the

General Staff developed and implemented the Schlieffen Plan and took upon itself the breach of Belgian neutrality with all its consequences. To promote a peace of understanding after the failure of the original war plan appears to me not as a political-moral contribution but rather as an effort to get out of the war, which turned out so differently than predicted by the German military, in a respectable way. But it was Bethmann Hollweg himself who made such a "peace of understanding" impossible for the nation because at the beginning of 1914 he presented the thesis of the "surprise attack" of the Entente upon Germany as the official interpretation of the outbreak of the war and derived from it the demand for "security and guarantees." How could this demand for security for the future now be surrendered if Germany had been attacked?!?!

3. In no way did Germany enter this war in order to conduct a "war of exhaustion" and achieve a "peace of understanding." Germany's conception was a lightning war and a lightning victory (in "total victory" as Ritter himself says). The readiness to renounce was only the consequence of the defeats at the Marne and in Flanders. But my book had as its starting point what Germany hoped to get from a decisive victory over France as well as finally over Russia, that is, from the question, how Europe would look if Germany had won the Battle of the Marne and attained the victorious peace for which she was striving. . . . The September Program provided the answer. . . . It may have been felt to be defensive, but it was offensive and expansive in its means. Ritter himself raises the question whether the German ordering of Europe contained in this program would have been bearable for the rest of the world . . . ; he even goes further than I and sees in it the seed of new wars. . . .

When it comes to the meaning of this program for German policy in the war, however, Ritter distorts the wording as well as the meaning of my book. Nowhere have I maintained that Bethmann Hollweg held "rigidly" to this program, or even that he saw in it an unconditional demand of German policy. Rather I said that the general line of "securing" Germany in the East and the West contained in it was maintained throughout the war, even if it was modified according to the military situation. (The astonishing thing is rather the extent to which Germany—here understood as the sum of all factors participating in the formation of the political will—held on to far reaching goals). Already in September 1914 Bethmann Hollweg had thrown his Central European Program onto the scales as an alternative to the most extreme demands, but he held to the intention of getting "securities"; whatever he may have personally thought, he had to hold on to it if he wanted to remain Chancellor of the German Empire. He was promptly overthrown when he deviated in foreign policy as well as in domestic policy from a line which was still bearable for those forces.

The nation's holding on to far reaching war aims was only made possible by Bethmann Hollweg, because he consciously did not enlighten the nation after September–November 1914 concerning the seriousness of the situation in order not to reduce their war efforts. He still believed he had to keep this policy in 1916–17 and it was continued by his successors until October 1918. Caught in the illusion of a still possible victory, the German people, or at least the dominant strata, held on to exaggerated (measured by the military situation) war aims. . . .

3a. Bethmann Hollweg and the Kreuznach war aims program of April 23, 1917. For the third time Gerhard Ritter repeats the incorrect contention that I ignored in my book an "important formal minute for the record" of the Chancellor, a minute which nullified his signature to the Kreuznach war aims program. . . . This minute is reported in my presentation, but I evaluate it in an entirely different way from Ritter. (It is a minute for history, like so many of those in the July 1914 crisis.) Bethmann Hollweg could not openly speak his mind neither to the Kaiser, nor to the Supreme Command, nor to the Reichstag. The notation was for him a means of justifying his actions to his conscience. . . . Ritter ascribes importance to the fact that the Chancellor . . . was confident that he could win over the Kaiser . . . for a moderation of German war aims as soon as a possibility of peace came into sight. But it was the Kaiser himself who, then, in May 1917 presented truly fantastic peace demands which went beyond the Kreuznach program, especially in the maritime area and in view of the exorbitant indemnities to be demanded of the Allies and America; it was the Kaiser, carried along by hopes for the success of unrestricted submarine warfare, who at that time was of the opinion that the English member of Parliament who would come to ask for peace would have to kneel down before the Imperial standard; and, what is more important, it was the

Kaiser himself who made impossible the . . . very distant hopes for a separate peace with the new liberal-democratic Russia . . . when he rudely demanded of his government, therefore the Reich Chancellor, that it keep to the war aims program which had been decided upon at the Kreuznach conference held under his (the Kaiser's) chairmanship. Here, therefore, lies a direct consequence of this program concerning which Bethmann Hollweg had made his minute for his conscience. Ritter is silent about that. . . .

34 COMMENT BY *Fritz Fellner*
(Salzburg)

. . . the conflict over details has allowed us to forget that the research work of Professor Ritter takes its point of departure from a basic position with which one must debate. The key to this position is given by that remark in the Rapport in which Professor Ritter reproaches the work of Professor Fischer for having misconstrued the so-called September program when he (i.e. Professor Fischer) understood it as a "grasp for world power." "It only demonstrates," so says Ritter, "the Chancellor's intention of forcefully destroying the ring of enemy alliances which had threatened the Central Powers for a long time and which had permitted Austria's Balkan war to become a European war." And at the close of his presentation Ritter opposes to Fischer's interpretation of the war aims policy as a "striving for German domination of the world" the view that in the policy of Bethmann Hollweg one is dealing with "measures of political conflict in the most extreme emergency."

Ritter, and with him many other historians, proves himself with these statements to be caught up in the conceptions of the political propaganda of that age. He takes over the slogans of encirclement and extreme emergency, as if Germany in those decades really faced in isolation an overwhelming aggressive alliance of the other great powers sworn to the destruction of Germany's integrity. For Ritter, the age of imperialism still remains the age of fighting leagues; alliances and leagues are placed in equal rank over against ententes, and thereby one conjures up the picture of two military camps presenting themselves for battle. But the incontestable German isolation of the first decade of the twentieth century developed from the failure to recognize every change which had characterized international relations in the prewar period. While the German statesmen and military leaders remained caught up in the ideas of alliances and cabinet wars, the other European great powers went over to a policy of ententes. While the German statesmen strove to acquire through alliances companions-in-arms for defensive or offensive conflict, the statesmen of Great Britain, France and Italy sought to compromise conflicting interests in ententes. The ententes of 1902, 1904 and 1907 served the adjustment of interests in Tripoli, Morocco and Persia. They were no "enemy alliances which had threatened the Central Powers for a long time." They served to divide the *world* into spheres of influence, but not the rule of the European *continent*. The German statesmen were repeatedly offered collaboration in this policy of ententes, and they—caught in the mentality of alliances—refused.

This insight is lacking in Ritter's presentation, just as it was lacking in the planning of German policy before and during the World War. He, like the then dominant statesmen and military leaders, lacks the insight to see that what he describes as an "expanded form of defence" was the ruthless destruction of a neighbor's rights to live. Ritter tries to explain Bethmann's position and temporary approval of extreme annexationist demands by arguing that he found himself in a personal as well as in a political situation of difficulty, since only in this way could he maintain himself in office and set back the even more extreme desires of the military. Yet Ritter shuts out the decisive insight that Bethmann's war aims were distinguished from those of a Ludendorff only in *degree* not in character. If Bethmann had really been against the war aims policy of the annexationists, then he had to draw the consequences. There have been German statesmen before Bethmann who in decisive moments of intoxication with victory intervened on the side of moderation against the military. The "constitutional position" of Bethmann was no worse than that of Bismarck.

Yet when Ritter at the end of his Rapport polemicizes against the influence of "certain politically fashionable currents," to which every form of German great power politics, even in the age of European imperialism, appears condemnable, then he surrenders the basis of his scholarly debate with the work of Fischer. He believes that out of a feeling of national solidarity he has to justify German policy even at a time when it was directed against the interests of the country and the people—just as at that time the best German thinkers and politicians, because of a feeling of national solidarity, did not dare to stand up against a misguided policy at a time when an open distancing of themselves (from this policy), when a decisive action of Bethmann's against the annexationists could have prevented the march into disaster. But with this the debate of Ritter with Fischer crosses over into the profound problem of German historical writing, a problem which a young German historian with whom I am closely befriended once correctly formulated with the words: It is the fate of German politics and historical science that only the year 1918 but not the year 1914 is viewed as a national catastrophe.

35 FROM *Wolfgang J. Mommsen*
The Debate on German War Aims

One of the most judicious appraisals of the debate over German war aims has been that of Wolfgang J. Mommsen, an outstanding German scholar who has written on the politics of Max Weber and on imperialism. He is now working on a biography of Bethmann Hollweg. The discussion below is critical of both Fischer and Ritter and takes a "middle" position. Nevertheless, it recognizes the significance of Fischer's work for both the war aims discussion and for German historiography in general

Fritz Fischer's large-scale study of the political war aims of imperial Germany from 1914–18 created a sensation on its ap-

SOURCE (33). Reprinted from Wolfgang J. Mommsen, "The Debate on German War Aims," *Journal of Contemporary History*, Vol. I, No. 3 (1966), with the permission of George Weidenfeld & Nicolson Ltd., pp. 47–72.

pearance in 1961 (since then there has already been a third, slightly amended edition) which was not confined to professional historians, but spread to the general public and has not yet subsided. The reason is clear; Fischer's inquiry touched one of the sore points of the German people's historical consciousness, which was just beginning to reawaken after the catastrophic end of the national-socialist era. Could it really be true that the whole of the recent German past, from the beginning of the twentieth century, was nothing more than the introductory phase of the "greater Germany" imperialism of the national-socialists? Fischer himself does not formulate the basic theses of his work very precisely; ideas like the one just mentioned appear, as it were, incidentally, but they force themselves on the reader's attention, not least by reason of his provocative and relentless style.

In point of fact, Fischer's propositions are put forward in the form of an inexorable deployment of evidence and thus constitute a formidable challenge to the traditional concept of the history of the first world war which, with only a few modifications, was accepted in their turn by German historians after 1945. In the Weimar period it was regarded as the duty of German historians to work for the revision of the war-guilt clause (para. 231 of the Versailles treaty), which formed the legal foundation of the whole structure of reparations and discriminations imposed on Germany. These efforts appeared on the whole to have been successful, and a kind of international consensus seemed to have been achieved to the effect that historical sources had not confirmed that Germany alone—her dubious policies of July 1914 notwithstanding—bore the burden of guilt for starting the war. Fischer does not agree with this view and, although using the conclusions reached in Luigi Albertini's great work on the policies of the European cabinets in July 1914, he exaggerates them to the point of declaring that German policy was, in fact, the decisive factor in provoking war, with the object of obtaining by force equality of status with the three great world powers—the British Empire, Tsarist Russia, and the United States. Germany's war aims, he contends, were not the outcome of the war situation, but rather a blatant expression of the German nation's will to world power and thus preceded the outbreak of war itself. Fischer rejects the explanation that these aims received their

final shape only under pressure of threats to the country's continental position. He presents instead a Germany engaged in a
continuous struggle for power—a struggle which, far from being
the result of an existing situation, was in fact the means by which
events were to be shaped. This interpretation is obviously based
largely on ethical convictions (although social, economic, and
political motivations are often brought into the argument), reflected in the repeated condemnation of the extremism and reck-
lessness of German nationalist and imperialist ambitions.

Previous research into this period did not ignore the popularity of extreme annexationist and imperialist views among large
sections of the German people, but this was mainly ascribed to
the war atmosphere and to the public's lack of information about
the true state of affairs. Insofar as annexationist aims were officially put forward, these were regarded as largely tactical moves
dictated by the military situation, or they were ascribed to the
military leaders. With the possible exception of the extreme left,
practically all groups were agreed that the government itself supported a comparatively moderate policy. This was not without
influence on the course of historical research, nor on the German
public's mental image of the events of that time.

What underlay this traditional interpretation of German policies? Contemporaries were clear in their own minds that the
German nation was at that time split into two warring camps,
on the one hand the supporters of the ideal of national self-suf-
ficiency, on the other the imperialists of the pan-German stamp.
Perhaps the most convincing account of this contemporary opinion is to be found in Ernst Troeltsch's courageous essay, published in the *Neue Rundschau* in the spring of 1915, that is to
say at a time when the battle in print about German war aims
had reached its first climax. Essentially, two irreconcilably hostile
forces confronted each other, the supporters of the traditional
ideal of the nation-state against the enthusiastic adherents of
imperialism. To the former the true purpose of the war was the
victorious defence of the German Reich against a world of enemies; hence their positive war aims were directed solely towards
ensuring the security of the empire: "such limitations in our
aims are forced upon us by the European balance of power, by
our geographical situation and its boundaries, by our past history, and above all by a deep ethical conviction which drives

us to achieve and maintain our own right of existence, but at the same time commands us to respect the independence of other nations and their own opportunities for genuine development." Naturally Troeltsch looked on himself as a member of this group. He summed up the attitude of its opponents: "What a German victory should aim to achieve is the permanent enfeeblement of the great world powers on its borders, namely the British and Russian empires; this would also remove for ever the French threat to Germany. German world power must supplant these weakened empires." This description of the war aims current at the time gives a fairly accurate picture of how the German people saw the situation, at least during the first years of the war. The annexationists in their turn also divided Germany into the same two camps, although using a very different vocabulary. They distinguished between those who possessed the will to power, the courage and toughness which were essential if a peace was to be won which would secure for all time Germany's position as a world power, and those others who, ensnared by humanitarian and sentimental illusions, failed to realize how serious the situation was and therefore pleaded for a "weak-kneed" peace.

Not surprisingly, Chancellor von Bethmann Hollweg in particular was regarded as a member of the anti-imperialist camp. From the start of the war it was generally agreed that Germany could sign a peace treaty only if it brought some recompense for the immense sacrifices that had been made. The consequence was an unending stream of expansionist war aims of a truly incredible extravagance, which came pouring out from almost every quarter. The Chancellor was, however, the soul of prudence, at any rate for the time being, and refused to take a public stand on this question; indeed, in the first months of the war he tried to discourage exaggerated nationalist expectations, so that almost from the start he gained the unenviable reputation of a defeatist and an anti-imperialist. On the other hand, the parties of the left, convinced that Bethmann Hollweg was no "blind annexationist," gave him their support.

Although as the war went on Bethmann was gradually forced to abandon discretion and to advance more or less unambiguous war aims, in the eyes of his right-wing critics he remained an unreliable fellow who was ready to renounce all annexationist claims if this would end the war. This was a point of view which —in spite of all the war-aims programmes discovered by Fritz Fischer—probably came very close to the Chancellor's inmost convictions. On the other side, the representatives of the left— with the exception of the insignificant Liebknecht group—continued until July 1917 to regard the Chancellor as an advocate of a compromise peace whom it was necessary to support in his struggle with the conservatives, despite the ambiguity of his declarations, public and private. Scheidemann's attempt in his speech at Breslau on 20 June 1916 to claim the Chancellor as his ally on the question of a peace without annexations was no doubt a good tactical move, but its success depended on the assumption that Bethmann Hollweg's efforts at negotiation on the basis of a peace without substantial annexations were genuine. It is clear that Scheidemann sincerely believed this, a belief that remained unshaken even after the war. Although exhorted to announce great and glorious war aims, which would arouse mass enthusiasm, the Chancellor continued to keep the door ajar for any possible development in the direction of negotiations, even in the face of a public opinion which in the main wanted annexations, and of a parliamentary majority united until July 1917 in its annexationist outlook. These tactics suggested that the Chancellor believed in a negotiated peace, but had not always managed to get his views accepted, an impression which received confirmation as he increasingly became the target of the military leaders.

The dispute determined the course of political events inside Germany in the later war years. Hence the attempt made retrospectively to distinguish between the "genuine" opponents of annexations and all those who to a greater or lesser extent departed from the aim of the *status quo ante* cannot be taken as a reliable guide for assessing the state of mind of the warring groups in Germany from 1914 to 1918. In fact, the formula which opposed the proponents of a "Hindenburg" peace to those of a "Scheidemann" peace continued to dominate public debate even after the war. In particular, it determined the course of the discussions of the Committee of Investigation set up by the Weimar National Assembly to examine the causes of Germany's defeat. Bethmann Hollweg and Jagow had little difficulty in heaping on the former military leadership the main responsibility for the extremist war-aims programmes of 1916 and 1917, which alone had been made public at the time. The Committee, almost every member of which detested Ludendorff, readily accepted this approach. Significantly, the members omitted to question Bethmann Hollweg more closely and agreed with him that "the virulent hatred with which the so-called annexationists hounded me" dispelled any doubts as to his attitude on war aims. When questioned about a conversation with the American ambassador, Gerard, in January 1917, during which he had informed the latter in a somewhat disguised form of Germany's current war aims, especially of the intention to maintain permanent indirect control of Belgium, Bethmann's reply was characteristic: "But Gerard knew that I . . . was no annexationist. The whole of Germany knew that." The ex-Chancellor had made a similar remark in a letter to Prince Max of Baden, written before the end of the war, which had come into the hands of the Committee of Investigation; "The world knows that I was never in favour of annexationism, and the proof is the hatred with which its apostles pursued me."

These testimonials to himself fitted well into the picture of the vehement disputes between the civil and military authorities about war aims and the conduct of internal affairs, which were still fresh in everyone's memory. The political climate of the post-war years, poisoned by the stab-in-the-back legend and the agitation concerning the war-guilt question, prevented a really objective view being taken of Germany's wartime policies. Bethmann Hollweg's undeniable bias in favour of a negotiated peace was entered far too quickly on the credit side of the war-guilt account, and the annexationist ambitions of official quarters, no secret at the time, were played down as being no more than concessions to the military leaders without any binding force.

Thus an image was created of a Chancellor who was a "lover of peace" and a "seeker after understanding," a man who had swum against the stream and stood up against the military. Otto Erich Volkmann, the expert attached to the Committee of Investigation, came to the conclusion that Bethmann "at any time during the course of the war would have consented to a peace which confirmed the *status quo ante*"; to be sure, he remarked

on another occasion that the ex-Chancellor's policies—in spite
of the fact that he was "inwardly" in favour of a negotiated
peace—had nonetheless scattered far and wide "the seeds of the
German policy of annexationism of the last war years." The attitude of the social-democrats contributed to the genesis of this
relatively favourable verdict on the Chancellor's policies.

This comparatively favourable image of Bethmann Hollweg
strongly influenced historical judgment on the period. Hitherto
neither contemporaries nor historians had doubted that up to
the time of their loss of effective power in the spring of 1917, the
political leaders had been in favour of a moderate negotiated
peace, whereas the military leaders, steeped in traditional concepts of a strategy of annihilation, had always striven for a peace
of absolute victory and had constantly been at odds with the civil
power on this question. Thus interest was concentrated on the
intense struggle which took place between the supporters of a
moderate peace and those of an overwhelmingly victorious
peace, one of the main purposes of which would be to destroy
England's mastery of the sea. In the opening years of the war
this struggle was waged in secret as a battle of dossiers, but from
the autumn of 1916 it was fought out in the open and with increasing bitterness. Yet very little was known publicly about
developments in foreign policy during the war, particularly the
numerous semi-official peace feelers that had been put out. Bethmann himself was generally regarded as a somewhat weak and
indecisive personality, well-intentioned but unable to assert himself against the combined opposition of the military establishment, conservative circles, industry, and the parties of the right;
there was general agreement that at any rate during his chancellorship, there had been no intention of making annexationist
demands that did not admit of compromise in the event of peace
negotiations; but there was not quite the same readiness to believe, as Volkmann did, that Bethmann Hollweg was prepared
to sign a negotiated peace that included no annexations of any
importance. Historical research has hitherto been inclined to attribute Germany's defeat to the succeeding Chancellors' abandonment of this moderate course under pressure from the
military leaders and the annexationist politicians of the right,
rather than to German policy on the outbreak of war and during

its first years. Thus the personality and the policies of the first wartime Chancellor were regarded up to 1918 as the keys to an understanding of the history of the first world war.

In his study of Germany's war aims in the West, Hans Gatzke had already made a breach in the wall of traditional interpretations, although he had had access only to printed source material. Nevertheless, he too maintained that the war aims of the government in general and of Bethmann Hollweg in particular were "on the whole moderate" in comparison with the extremist plans propagated among the German public. But it was Fritz Fischer, later backed up by Werner Basler and Imanuel Geiss, who was the first to abandon the conventional pattern of two sharply contrasted camps, one annexationist, the other moderate and basically non-annexationist, substituting for it the thesis of the "fundamental unanimity of will with regard to war aims that characterized all politically influential circles in Germany from the Kaiser himself, by way of the civil government and the military leadership, right down to the Reichstag majority and the German press." His examination leads Fischer to the conclusion that the differences of attitude were of only limited significance even though contemporaries may have felt them very deeply. Variations of opinion, whether in official circles or outside, were, he maintains, of little importance in face of that monolithic will to world power shared by all the influential groups and classes of the nation. To be sure, Fischer also points out that it was principally the army, heavy industry, and wide sections of the upper middle class which championed the most outrageous of the imperialist war aims; but the Social-Democratic Party and those members of the German intelligentsia who during the later stages of the war were the guiding spirits behind the "People's Union for Freedom and Fatherland," are also found guilty of having lent temporary support to Germany's claim to world rule or, at any rate, world power. Thus, e.g. Ernst Troeltsch, Friedrich Meinecke, and Alfred Weber are implicitly counted among the imperialists, although not among the open ones. Only the extreme left and certain out-and-out pacifists like Friedrich Wilhelm Foerster can measure up to Fischer's inflexible yardstick of probity—support for the absolute *status quo ante*.

In point of fact Fischer goes even beyond this. He does not

confine himself to asserting that the antagonism between imperialists and so-called anti-imperialists was superficial; he states
that the leaders of the Reich—not only the Kaiser and the High
Command, but specifically also Bethmann Hollweg and his closest collaborators—were united in their resolve to extend Germany's power at the expense of each one of her enemies, that
this resolve was faithfully, fully, and above all unbrokenly pursued during the whole course of the war, and that in view of this
basic agreement the numerous conflicts between them are of secondary importance. In spite of differences of outlook on certain
points, Fischer argues, they were united in working for the ag-
grandisement of German power and regarded this as the true
object of the war. This very rigid black and white thesis is derived from a mass of documentary records and is presented as
the actual and factual core of all the confusing quarrels between parties and groups and government departments of every
shape and kind. The most important part of the argument is the
attempt to prove that the views of the political leaders did not
differ significantly from those of the military leaders but that,
on the contrary, their common aim of fighting for German world
power was in complete harmony with the desires of the overwhelming majority of the German people.

This presentation of the facts, whose objective accuracy is not
under discussion at the moment, not only contrasts sharply with
the traditional portrait of Bethmann Hollweg as the statesman
of moderation and compromise, but is also the complete antithesis of the earlier views discussed above about the whole complex of German war-aims policies. According to Fischer, the
entire German nation, with the exception of some small and unimportant groups, had to a greater or lesser degree become the
victims of an overwhelming obsession with power, the desire to
obtain for the German empire equality of status with the three
great world powers. Fischer describes the first wartime Chancellor as a clear-headed politician who deliberately led Germany
into the war and thereafter, while remaining flexible in his methods, worked tenaciously and unyieldingly for the expansion of
German power. He seems bent on a complete reversal of those
views on Bethmann Hollweg which had developed in the atmosphere of the struggle against the charge of war guilt, as of
a man who was always "prepared to negotiate," but who had

been frustrated by an unfortunate conjunction of political obstacles. This interpretation is as mistaken as the earlier ones, since it once again reduces the whole question of Bethmann's war-aims policies to a matter of "political attitudes," to a purely personal, patient, and unremitting effort to enhance Germany's power both eastwards and westwards. All the Chancellor's actions are inspected in this light, and when they do not fit the pattern they are said to have been modified for tactical reasons only—a method used in the traditional interpretations, but in reverse. To this is added the further thesis of the continuity of Germany's war-aims policies, from September 1914 right up to the 1918 treaties with the enemies in eastern Europe. This, too, is contrary to general opinion, which sees the transition to unlimited submarine warfare and the complete military takeover of both home and foreign affairs by Hindenburg and Ludendorff as a fundamental change of direction in war policy.

In general, Fischer reaches his conclusions by assessing attitudes and virtually disregarding differences of circumstance. The political actions of the persons and groups governing Germany during the first world war are attributed to their ethical outlook, measured in relation to specific principles of power politics, imperialism, etc., while all the external factors which may have influenced them are more or less ignored. Fischer and his pupil Geiss seem to be concerned above all to expose as unmistakably as possible an attitude of mind which they rightly detest; hence their obvious tendency to exploit to the limit the documents relating to war aims and to ignore the fact that in politics no less than in daily life deeds seldom match up to words. Fischer shows no interest in the greater or lesser differences of attitude hidden behind the positions adopted in public for tactical reasons by the different government departments and personalities. He confines himself to the literal wording of the documents, whatever the situation in which they were composed and whatever the specific object they served. In certain cases, as for instance the treatment of the war-aims conference at Kreuznach on 23 April 1917, the use of this method is particularly irritating, since it must be taken for granted that in politics points of view which are fundamentally different in their nature are practically always presented as being merely different in degree.

Moreover, Fischer is bent on producing not so much a narrative of events or reconstructing the chain of cause and effect, as a continual stream of new evidence for the sole purpose of proving his main theme—Germany's will to unlimited world power. Although it would be absurd and unjust to accuse Fischer of conscious tampering with the sources, there are in his work many exaggerated and biased statements (some of which were subsequently withdrawn). For instance, he regards the German peace offer of 12 December 1916 as nothing more than a trick, the purpose of which was to hinder Wilson's inconvenient attempts at mediation and to make diplomatic preparations for unrestricted submarine warfare, whereas it is perfectly obvious that Bethmann Hollweg meant this offer quite seriously and, although he was not very optimistic about its chance of success, regarded it as the final attempt to avert the *ultima ratio* of the submarine war.

Thus, in spite of the profusion of source material which he for the first time made available to historical research, an achievement which merits unreserved recognition, Fischer's interpretation is open to attack on many points. But this does not fully explain why the discussion about his theories aroused so much heat, at any rate in its early stages. The reason is that his conclusions, put forward perhaps hastily, are in sharp contrast to the contemporary image of the period, which still influences our own historical consciousness. His work heralded a change in the character of our politico-historical thought. Attitudes which seemed to contemporaries consistent with the maintenance of the status quo and thus purely defensive in principle, have today the appearance of out-and-out annexationism or at the least of some variety of indirect rule. This conclusion is reinforced when German war aims are considered in isolation and not in relation to the war aims of the Allies. Fischer's tendency to ignore power-political concepts to the point of denying them altogether, and his measurement of German war-aims policy by the standard of a complete territorial *status quo ante,* make nonsense of the history of the late Wilhelmian era; nowhere, it seems, is intelligent insight to be found; on every hand there is nothing but boundless, utopian nationalism, often tinged with *völkisch* ideas. Nor does he even consider this as due in part to the war atmosphere, which has at all times and everywhere had the effect of stirring up nationalist sentiments. On the contrary, he makes the war itself appear to be the outcome of this delusionary nationalist struggle for world power. Is the history of the late Wilhelmian era really nothing more than the introductory phase of the national-socialist hankering after world conquest? And was the Social-Democratic Party's celebrated declaration of loyalty to their country on 4 August 1914 also nothing more than a mixture of crude self-deception and unacknowledged nationalist imperialism?

It is these implications in Fischer's writing which account for the sometimes very harsh reviews of his work. Had all the efforts to reach an objective clarification of the war-guilt question been meaningless and misdirected? Had Germany deliberately brought about not only the second but also the first world war? These questions are not discussed in detail by Fischer himself, but to the general public they seemed to constitute the quintessence of his argument. This of course opened up old wounds at a time when Germans were trying to understand their own historical past, and it is not surprising that this reaction gave rise in its turn to a series of unedifying feuds in the press.

A scholarly discussion of Fischer's theories had already begun before the appearance of *Griff nach der Weltmacht,* for he had made known his main conclusions in pre-publication extracts in the *Historische Zeitschrift.* Hans Herzfeld immediately questioned Fischer's views on Bethmann Hollweg. Using the diaries of Admiral Müller and the memoirs of Friedrich Meinecke, he pointed out how very moderate the Chancellor's attitude actually was, considering the heavy pressures to which he was subjected; he also doubted whether it was legitimate to talk about an unbroken line of German war-aims policy since August 1914. Shortly after, Gerhard Ritter attacked Fischer's interpretation of German policy in the July crisis in an unusually sharply-worded article. Subsequently the controversy spread to ever wider circles, as new aspects of the problem were revealed by further research. The subject is now too vast to be covered in a single article.

So far discussion has been concentrated in the main on two groups of problems: first, the causes of the war and the closely connected question of how far German war aims were foreshadowed in the policies of the pre-war years; second, the assessment of the war-aims policies themselves.

Given the importance which German historians in the twenties and thirties attached to the war-guilt question, it is not surprising that Fischer's pronouncements on German policy in the July crisis immediately aroused general attention and sharp opposition. His view that the ideas put forward by Friedrich v. Bernhardi in *Deutschland und der nächste Krieg,* published in 1912, rendered "with absolute precision the intentions of official Germany," although the German Foreign Office, for one, tried at the time to have them rejected, provoked vigorous criticism in many quarters as an overstatement of an undeniable fact. Another of his theses that could not stand up to examination, at any rate in the form in which it was presented, was his assertion that the German political leadership, relying on British neutrality, was bent at the very least on inflicting a severe humiliation on Russia on the Balkan question, but was prepared to start a four-power war for the hegemony of Europe, in which England was expected to stand aside. It was pointed out in several quarters that if Germany became involved in a general war, then in the given circumstances it would automatically be waged against France, and Bethmann Hollweg fully expected that England in this event would join the enemy side, though perhaps not necessarily from the very beginning. In view of this, one of the key assumptions of Fischer's original interpretation of German diplomacy in the July crisis falls away. In his introduction to the third volume of his *Staatskunst und Kriegshandwerk,* Ritter once again, in opposition to Fischer, identified the subordination of the political establishment to the military leaders as the decisive cause of the failure to preserve peace. Over and above this, he holds fast to his belief in the basically defensive character of German policy. This is a view accepted by Karl Dietrich Erdmann as well, since he became acquainted with the diaries kept by Bethmann Hollweg's private secretary Riezler. To be sure, Erdmann has now conceded, contrary to his earlier view, that by 5 July 1914, the Chancellor was already fully conscious of the possibility of a general war breaking out in which England too would be involved. On the other hand, Egmont Zechlin has lately attempted to explain Germany's conduct in the July crisis as arising from secret information about a naval treaty between Russia and England that was said to be in course of preparation and which aroused fears of a closer alliance of the two powers. He considers that this ever-threatening danger of England taking sides with Germany's continental rivals, a step which was bound to have a catastrophic effect on Bethmann's long-term foreign policies, was the reason why the Reich, literally at the last moment and at the risk of world war, started a political offensive. Its purpose was both to give effective support to her only remaining ally, Austria-Hungary, and to force a show-down about the Balkan crisis that had been looming over Europe for years, at a moment still relatively favourable to Germany. These interpretations do approximate to Fischer's point of view, since they agree on the growth of an attitude of fatalism, the belief that "war will come for all that" which undoubtedly affected the decisions of Germany's political leaders, and also admit that the thought of a preventive war entered as one element into their political calculations. Meanwhile, Imanuel Geiss, a pupil of Fritz Fischer, has compiled a collection of documents in two volumes, consisting with few exceptions of material already to be found in official publications, but with a very full commentary frankly designed to give documentary confirmation to Fischer's case. It is a pity that the sole aim of this documentation is to throw light on the decisions of the German government, the diplomatic documents of the other powers concerned being included as it were as a mere sideline.

Latterly, however, Fischer has been rather letting his defenders down by becoming more and more radical in his views concerning Germany's responsibility for the outbreak of the war. In a lengthy essay in the *Historische Zeitschrift,* completed in 1963 but not published until 1964, he not only defends his previous ideas, but tries to strengthen his case by attributing Germany's decision to make war to the effects of a crisis in the development of her economic expansion in south-east Europe. The demonstration is unconvincing because there is no direct connection between the failure of German attempts at economic expansion in Greece, Bulgaria, and Turkey, and the decision of 5 July 1914 to give unconditional support to Austria-Hungary in the Serbian question. This decision must be considered as a complete reversal of the German Foreign Office's previous attitude, which had however already been undermined to some extent by Wilhelm's declarations to Archduke Ferdinand during his visit to Vienna in March 1913, under the pressure of military quarters. Economic issues do not seem to have affected it in any way.

But this is not all. Fischer took up an even more intransigent stand in a long article published in *Die Zeit* of 3 September 1965, in which he asserted that since 1913 Germany had been systematically making preparations to launch a world war: "By the summer of 1914 the war had been well prepared intellectually, politically, diplomatically, and economically! All that remained to be done was to actually bring it about," and for this purpose the assassination at Sarajevo came at the right moment. A little later, in a volume of the series entitled *Weltmacht oder Untergang. Deutschland im 1. Weltkrieg,* Fischer again spoke out (this was obviously written before the article in *Die Zeit,* but appeared later). Here his tone was somewhat more moderate; "Germany deliberately made use of the Sarajevo incident as an opportunity for overcoming the obstacles to German world-power policies." Granted the close connection between the longing of the German people in the years before the war to win successes in world politics and German policy after Sarajevo, do the sources confirm his main thesis, namely that the government of the Reich had since 1913 deliberately steered a course towards war because it considered that all prospects for a peaceful enhancement of Germany's world status had been blocked? Fischer is now preparing a new book in which he intends to supply the proof for this assertion; it is to be called *Der Krieg der Illusionen,* and is awaited with some eagerness. Nevertheless, the feeling remains that this radicalization of his opinions lessens the persuasive power of his arguments. Even granted that the German government since 1906 (the rights and wrongs of its actions are here not under discussion) felt itself compelled to embark on policies which steadily increased the risk of war, the theory that long before Sarajevo German statesmen were already determined to embark on a general war as an escape from their difficulties does not seem convincing, especially as there is general agreement that Bethmann himself was opposed to a preventive war. His original plan, certainly after 1912, was to edge cautiously towards an agreement with Russia and also and especially with England. He did not, as Fischer seems to assume, expect to achieve by this means an immediate increase of political elbow-room, but only a gradual improvement of the general political climate, in order to open up long-term prospects of success in the field of world politics. Argument will also go on as to the justification for at-

tributing one and all of the 1914 German war aims to political
and economic aspirations of the pre-war period. Certainly the war
aims of 1914 did not just fall from the sky; but the mere fact that
they were given concrete shape only during the 1914 "state of
siege" should surely be a warning against over-hasty back-dating.

Hitherto, when historians have asserted that in the years before
the war Germany was mainly interested in economic expansion,
they have based their opinion largely on the Ruedorffer-Riezler
book *Grundzüge der Weltpolitik* (1914). Now that Erdmann has
gone to the pages of the Riezler diary (unfortunately still not
available for general use), to illustrate the comparative moderation of Bethmann Hollweg's policies, Riezler has also been drawn
into the controversy. Imanuel Geiss has lately tried to prove that
Riezler was most probably in favour of a war as a means of
cutting the Gordian knot of world politics. It was the same
Riezler who, during the first world war, as confirmed by the
same sources, was attacked by Dietrich Schaefer as the protagonist
of a feeble pacifism. More convincing is the approach of Hill-
gruber, who recently tried to distil from Riezler's writings a
theory of the risks of war in the age of modern power politics
which may have guided Bethmann Hollweg and his counsellors
in the critical days of July 1914. Yet, however Riezler's diary is
interpreted, one thing is incontrovertible, namely the alarming
spirit of fatalism in which wide circles of the German (and indeed not only the German) public, as well as their political
leaders, awaited the approaching war. This was a frame of mind
that, when the hour of crisis came, decisively weakened the will
to preserve peace.

We now reach the second big group of problems—the evalua-
tion of the policies followed by Germany during the war itself.
Here the difficulties of trying to present a complete picture of the
many different views which have been put forward during the
discussion of Fischer's theses are even greater. An attempt will
nevertheless be made to give at least a short summary of the
different points of view which have emerged.

Criticism of Fischer's work was at first mainly concerned with
his conception of the personality and policies of Chancellor
Bethmann Hollweg. It is to Fischer's lasting credit that he was
the first to survey the whole range of war-aims programmes drawn

up by the various government departments on the Chancellor's instructions. But in his eagerness to give them an exact and pithy description, he went too far, at least in certain respects, in his opposition to the views that had prevailed hitherto. Even otherwise favourable reviews, such as Klaus Epstein's, questioned Fischer's ready acceptance, as proof of his own opinion, of remarks made to third parties by Bethmann, although it was quite obvious that these only showed that he was deliberately being 'all things to all men'. Fischer's portrait of Bethmann Hollweg as a statesman steadily pursuing far-reaching power-political and imperialist aims, misses the essence of the Chancellor's personality. Even on the question of war aims he was always seeking points of agreement, and at the beginning of the war at least he tried to damp down the exaggerated expectations of the over-excited masses. In a penetrating study based on the Riezler diaries, Erdmann has recently described the great gulf between Bethmann and the Pan-Germans and their middle-class and conservative supporters with their naive aspirations.

Janssen, too, in his brilliant book about the war-aims policies of the German federal states, draws special attention to the Chancellor's comparatively moderate political line. And even Willibald Gutsche, an East German historian, attests in Bethmann's favour that his war aims were in conformity with the tendencies of the more moderate group within "German monopoly capitalism," and that he was sharply opposed to the aims of heavy industry, which enjoyed the support of Bissing, governor-general of Belgium. It can hardly be denied that Fischer limits his inquiry strictly to an exposure of Germany's struggle for power and does not give adequate consideration to the political difficulties which the Chancellor and his colleagues faced at home vis-à-vis both the general public and the military establishment. This situation forced them continually to temporize and to change their tactics. To those who have studied the sources it is disturbing that Bethmann Hollweg's bitter opposition to the Pan-Germans and the industrialists and ultra-conservatives behind them, which greatly increased his difficulties, is dealt with by Fischer as if it were of merely secondary importance. There was after all a world of difference between Bethmann's September Programme and Class's first big memorandum on war aims; it is misleading to suggest that the two are identical in attitude. In reply, Fischer argues with much justice that the question is not so much one of Bethmann Hollweg's personal views but rather of his political activities, and that he could not have acted otherwise than he did. To prove this it would be necessary to supplement the analysis of Bethmann's personality and political strategy by a study in depth of the whole contemporary political system. Fischer makes a valuable start in this direction, but only a start, due to his predilection for explanations based on political attitudes and socio-economic laws.

Efforts of the same nature are to be found in Egmont Zechlin's numerous, discerning, but unfortunately widely-dispersed papers. He is mainly concerned to show that Bethmann's policy was a "cabinet" policy in the style of the nineteenth century, tuned from the first to a limited war followed by a peace negotiated between cabinets, public opinion being as far as possible excluded. He tries to make out, not always convincingly, that Bethmann Hollweg at first took the line that England would show restraint in the military field and might even be prepared to act as mediator, until he was forced to recognize that England intended to fight to a finish. He shows that the question of how the struggle against England was to be carried on in the event of a French defeat was of great importance in the genesis of the so-called September Programme. Indeed, there can hardly be a doubt that the *Vorläufige Richtlinien über unsere Politik beim Friedensschluss* implicitly rest on the assumption that England would go on with the war (as emerges also from the Chancellor's accompanying letter to Delbrück of 9 September 1914), otherwise it would be astonishing that England, in the eyes of the German public the main enemy, is not even mentioned in a Programme in which, according to Fischer, the basic aims of German policy for the whole course of the war are spelled out. In view of Rechenberg's catalogue of demands to France concerning rights in Channel ports and so forth for the duration of the war, which was obviously drawn up in the light of the September Programme, and of the stock-phrase 'continental blockade' in Riezler's diary, it must have been drawn up, at least in part, as a programme for the war against England. For even after a French defeat, which at the time the Germans regarded as imminent, England and its Dominions were expected to carry on the war, or at least to deny Germany access to the open sea for the foreseeable future. Neither the September programme, nor the other private or public statements by the Chancellor, too numerous to be dealt with here in detail, can be said to have quite the conclusive force as regards his personal views on war aims that Fischer attributes to them; but it must be admitted, in Fischer's favour, that Bethmann Hollweg, moderate as he was, was not in a position to get his line of policy accepted in other government quarters. Whatever risks the Chancellor was prepared to take in flouting both official and public opinion, as in his readiness to cede a small part of Silesia to facilitate agreement between Vienna and Rome, he could never have prevailed against the more or less annexationist majority of the nation, and particularly the military. Perhaps he shrank from open battle on behalf of his moderate views, as was stated after his fall by Eugen Schiffer, a personal friend; or again, the power of the military establishment to extend its influence far beyond the limits of its own sphere of activities made such an outcome impossible. It is mainly to the elucidation of this last question that Gerhard Ritter devotes the third volume of his *Staatskunst und Kriegshandwerk*. This is a detailed study of the war years during which Bethmann Hollweg was Chancellor, and an admirably comprehensive summing-up of the results of recent research. Compared with Fischer's methods, it has the great advantage of being a lucid narrative, dealing also with the policies of the Allies and of the United States. Ritter as well as Fischer was able to make use of a great deal of unpublished official material, and also of a new edition of the files of German Foreign Office documents concerning Germany's efforts for a separate peace. In contrast to Fischer, Ritter maintains that German policies were originally basically defensive in nature. He does not deny that in the course of the war they took on a more offensive character as efforts were made to strengthen and extend Germany's power on the Continent, either indirectly by economic hegemony or directly by open annexation; but he is far milder than Fischer in his interpretation of German war policy as a whole.

Fundamentally, the conclusions reached by the two writers are nonetheless not all that dissimilar. Ritter also believes that the "unsolved 'Belgian question' . . . became the curse of Germany's whole war policy." But, unlike Fischer, he tries to show that there was some justification in Germany's attempt to acquire some form of permanent control over Belgium. Using King Albert's diary, he throws new light on the 1916 negotiations on Belgium (which Fischer was the first to present in detail), showing that there actually was a real chance of indirectly fitting the Belgian glacis into the German sphere of influence (although the question arises whether negotiations with a monarch that were taking place against the declared wish of the Belgian government could really have led to a permanent solution acceptable to both sides). Bethmann Hollweg took these hopes so seriously that in his catalogue of German war aims prepared for Wilson at the end of January 1917 he asked, on the Belgian question, only for a free hand to settle it by bilateral agreement with King Albert. With regard to a peace settlement on the eastern front, Ritter's conclusions are once again more moderate than Fischer's. Bethmann, he says, believed "national hopes of territorial acquisition should never stand in the way of a separate peace with Russia." But this leaves certain questions unanswered, for example the extent of the annexations desired by Germany, and the degree to which even limited territorial claims, such as the Polish border strip, were an obstacle to a separate peace with Russia. There is in our view no doubt whatever that the High Command and the Kaiser were determined in 1917 to block any peace negotiations with Russia that assumed German renunciation of any large-scale annexations. This was a situation which Bethmann regretted, and which fatally compromised his position; but he did not openly resist.

Ritter's actual theme is, of course, the influence of the military establishment on political decisions, and here he is in full accord with earlier opinion, and perhaps goes further than is appropriate in emphasizing the point. Yet his approach is anything but conventional; in his appraisal of Falkenhayn and Ludendorff he carries out a noteworthy "revaluation of values." In complete contrast to the earlier literature, he draws a surprisingly favourable portrait of Falkenhayn, whereas Hindenburg and Ludendorff are painted in the blackest colours. Ritter praises not only Falkenhayn's comparatively moderate attitude in the war-aims question, but also his military strategy. This has traditionally been regarded as mistaken because of the failure of the great offensives at Ypres and Verdun, with their frightful casualties. Ritter maintains that there were only slight differences of opinion about war aims between Falkenhayn and Bethmann Hollweg; together they formed "a united front against the tumultuous nationalism, 'militarism,' and annexationism of public opinion," and he is surprised that no closer relationship ever developed between the two. It is true that military anxieties and difficulties weighed heavily on Falkenhayn and explain his moderate attitude; but he was an extremely ambitious man with great influence on the Kaiser, and Bethmann had to be continually on the watch to frustrate the Chief of Staff's political proposals. The rumour circulating at that time that Falkenhayn was about to become Chancellor was not altogether without foundation. His efforts to force a separate peace with Russia and his attitude on the submarine question repeatedly endangered the Chancellor's position. In the end it was Bethmann Hollweg himself who caused Falkenhayn's fall and who did not hesitate to use the weapon of prolonged and patient intrigue to bring this about, when he realized that a peace settlement could not be reached in partnership with the general. Since the hard core of Ritter's account is an analysis of the antagonism between the political and military leaders, he criticizes Fischer for treating this question as secondary to the combined will of both sides to extend the power of the Reich to the utmost limits of what was possible.

This is certainly justified to some extent. On some points, however, he definitely overstates his case. For instance, the great crisis of confidence in the year 1917, of which Bethmann finally became the victim, was in point of fact less the result of soldiers dabbling in politics than the outcome of the deep disappointment at the failure of unrestricted submarine warfare, which German propaganda had presented as the "infallible weapon" to bring the war to an end by summer at the very latest.

One other aspect of Ritter's book is also unsatisfactory—its marked anti-Austrian tone. It would seem that Ritter succumbed to the temptation to present German policies in a more favourable light by giving them, as a dark background, the partly defeatist, partly annexationist, and wholly dishonest conduct of the Emperor Charles and his foreign secretary Count Czernin. Ritter's assumption that there was a strong tendency in Vienna to conclude a separate peace with the Entente at the expense of her German ally is not confirmed by Wolfgang Steglich in his recent detailed study, *Politics of Peace of the Central Powers*

1917–18. Steglich does not gloss over the far-reaching annexationist aims of the Central Powers even in those years; nonetheless he arrives at the challenging conclusion that they might have agreed to a *Behauptungsfrieden* that was tantamount to a peace on the basis of the *status quo ante,* but that the Western Powers would not have agreed, since a negotiated peace by which Germany's status as a Great Power would have been acknowledged almost unimpaired, would have broken up the Entente.

No doubt this is not the last word in the debate on German policies during the first world war. The process of re-examining traditional concepts has been intensified and is being extended far beyond the problems of those years. The younger generation of German historians is striving, in a much more unbiased and critical state of mind than hitherto, to identify the sources of infection in German society which provided the seed-bed for the rise of national-socialism. Seen in this light, Fischer's studies have certain great and lasting merits. They have shattered some traditional beliefs and taboos, and directed historical research into new paths, and it is therefore a matter for regret that official government quarters have frowned on Fischer's theses and have attempted, if only indirectly, to hinder their dissemination. It may also be doubted whether it was proper to reprint in the official Government bulletin the article entitled "Die Last des Vorwurfs: Zweimal deutsche Kriegsschuld?," in which Eugen Gerstenmaier gives his wholly negative views on Fischer's theses. The manner in which official quarters took sides, until the daily press exposed their attitude, met with general disapproval by the German historians, even those highly critical of Fischer.

None of the protagonists in this heated debate denies that a thorough revision of the opinions held hitherto has now become necessary. To be sure opinions are divided as to how far such a revision should go. The theoretical basis of the discussion seems to be changing ground and moving gradually towards what in the long run could become a closer approximation of the different points of view. The argumentation of Fischer and his school is increasingly based on economic and social history, aspects of the question hitherto virtually ignored except by Kehr, Hallgarten, and Vagts. Yet much of the preparatory work in this field still remains to be done. The recent contributions from East Germany are not altogether satisfying owing to the pre-arranged explanatory pattern usually employed over there.

It is noteworthy that it is the communist historians, too, who do not approve of some of Fischer's conclusions, though they welcome his exposure of the nationalistic antecedents of non-communist Germany. For Fischer does not place the whole burden of responsibility for Germany's far-reaching war aims on the shoulders of the so-called ruling and upper middle classes, especially the big industrialists, and this does not fit into the Marxist-Leninist pattern. Furthermore, he does not in their view lay enough stress on the opposition of the extreme left to the imperialist policy of the "ruling classes." On the contrary, he presents the socialist workers either as the "fellow travellers" of government policy, or, in so far as they openly declared war on the latter, he simply dismisses them as having had little influence on the course of events. Moreover, Fischer implies that Germany bears, if not the sole, at all events the greatest share of the guilt for the outbreak of the war and for its pursuit to the point of utter exhaustion, in contrast to the Marxist-Leninist view, in which all capitalist states are inexorably driven to war.

In West German research there is a growing tendency to examine the domestic German situation to discover why, in 1914–18, German war aims were so unrealistic. The constitutional, political, and social structure of the German Empire, which was at that time passing through a period of crisis, must obviously provide a large part of the explanation, and Fischer recently asserted that German expansionist aims during the war were designed to preserve the "traditional class and social structure of the Prusso-German Reich" in face of the mounting pressures of democracy. This is a tenable thesis, but in the loose and general formulations in which Fischer clothes it, it is neither very new nor very informative. Even at the time it was clearly realized, among others by Max Weber, that there was a direct connection between the extreme annexationist aims of the Right and the social and economic interests of their own group. One of the main future tasks of historical research will be to define and classify these interests more precisely and to analyse them within the framework of the political and social conditions of the last years of the Wilhelmian Reich. A beginning has already been made in the work of Reinhard Patemann, Willibald Gutsche,

Pogge-Strandmann, and Egmont Zechlin. One may hope that as research on these questions expands, the general discussion will gain in objectivity. Opinions on Germany's policies in the first world war have clashed with such unaccustomed bitterness because, during the years of national-socialist rule, students of German contemporary history were prevented from treating these burning questions of the immediate German past in an impartial and unprejudiced manner. And so the prejudices, opinions, and attitudes of contemporaries were kept alive in their original form, instead of undergoing the customary continuous process of revision. The debate on German war aims is itself a symptom of the fact that the Germans, because of the crises and upheavals in their history since 1918, have not yet found their way back to an undivided historical consciousness.

SUGGESTIONS FOR FURTHER READING

Since a full-scale bibliography of the literature on war aims in the First World War would be extraordinarily long and almost entirely in German, no attempt will be made here to cover the field. Instead, the brief suggestions below will go beyond the immediate subject of this collection in an effort to place the war aims controversy in the perspective of recent writings on German foreign policy, although it will be limited to important collections and works in English in dealing with the war aims literature itself.

It should be clear that Fritz Fischer's work on war aims in the First World War is part of a much larger reevaluation of Germany's role in world affairs. An important impulse in the direction of such a reevaluation was provided in a series of essays published in the early 1950s by Ludwig Dehio and now collected in *Germany and World Politics in the Twentieth Century* (New York, 1967). Since the appearance of the works of Dehio and Fischer, critical studies dealing with more specialized periods have appeared. Helmut Böhme's *Deutschlands Weg zur Grossmacht* (Cologne and Berlin, 1966) investigates the relationship between economics and politics in the founding of the German Empire and for the period 1848–1881, while Hans-Ulrich Wehler's *Bismarck und der Imperialismus* (Cologne, 1969) brilliantly reexamines the foundations of Bismarckian imperialism. Fischer himself has recently moved back into the immediate prewar period with his massive *Krieg der Illusionen. Die deutsche Politik, 1911–14* (Düsseldorf, 1969). Fischer's concern with demonstrating Germany's war guilt has been seconded by Immanuel Geiss, whose two volume publication of documents on the outbreak of the war has now appeared in a condensed English

219

version as *July 1914. The Outbreak of the First World War: Selected Documents* (London, 1967). The most sensible and careful analysis of Germany's responsibility is Konrad H. Jarusch, "The Illusion of Limited War: Bethmann Hollweg's Calculated Risk, July 1914," *Central European History,* Vol. II, No. 1 (March 1969).

Two excellent collections of articles on the war aims question are Ernst W. Graf von Lynar, editor, *Deutsche Kriegsziele 1914–1918* (Darmstadt, 1964) and Wolfgang Schieder, *Erster Weltkrieg. Ursachen, Entstehung und Kriegsziele (Neue Wissenschaftliche Bibliothek, No. 32)* (Cologne and Berlin, 1969). Both contain excellent and very full bibliographies, which should be consulted by those wishing to pursue this problem further. The Schieder collection also has the advantage of presenting essays on the war aims of the other European powers. Those limited to the use of English sources may consult a number of works in addition to those of Rosenberg, Wheeler-Bennett, Gatzke, and Fischer used in this collection. See the late Klaus Epstein's "The Development of German-Austrian War Aims in the Spring of 1917," *Journal of Central European Affairs,* 17 (April 1957), his *Matthias Erzberger and the Dilemma of German Democracy* (Princeton, 1959), and his review of the first German edition of Fischer's *Griff nach der Weltmacht,* "German War Aims in the First World War," *World Politics,* 15 (October 1962).

The *Mitteleuropa* question receives an important treatment in Henry Cord Meyer, *Mitteleuropa in German Thought and Action, 1815–1945* (The Hague, 1955). An excellent discussion of the Bethmann Hollweg problem is provided by Fritz Stern's "Bethmann Hollweg and the War: The Limits of Responsibility," in Leonard Krieger and Fritz Stern, editors, *The Responsibility of Power. Historical Essays in Honor of Hajo Holborn* (New York, 1967). Although primarily concerned with the socioeconomic history of wartime Germany, Gerald D. Feldman, *Army, Industry and Labor in Germany, 1914–1918* (Princeton, 1966) does contain some new material of relevance to the war aims problem.[1] Finally, for a brilliant and stimulating analysis of the

---

[1] For a review of Fischer more favorable than that of Mommsen on the question of war aims but much more critical on the question of methodology, see the review written by the editor of this collection in *Journal of Modern History,* 41 (June 1969), pp. 260–267.

relationship between war aims and domestic politics on a European scale, see Arno J. Mayer, *Political Origins of the New Diplomacy, 1917–1918* (New Haven, 1959).